AF364626

Joyfulness

From looking in to looking after

Moving on from Mindfulness

Johan Spaans

2019

Joyfulness® has been registered as a trademark by

VOF Andere Wereld, Welsum (Olst-Wijhe), the Netherlands

Translation: Lizzie Kean

Photos: Lydia Knoop

Cover: Carianne van Raak and Lydia Knoop

Illustration *Andere Wereld*: Rob Otterspeer

Publisher: Johan Spaans, 2019, Welsum, The Netherlands

ISBN: 9789083034201

NUR: 728; 808

BISAC: OCC019000, BUS046000, SEL03100

CONTENTS

Preface

If you want to experience a zest for life (Joy) in these hectic times, you will have to go on a journey of discovery, a journey which will take you from looking in to looking after. The first thing you will notice is that you don't get far on this journey if you are travelling alone. The current culture of 'me, me, me' and the emphasis on individual performance really get in the way of Joy. There are too many people who have lost their Joy and are experiencing depression or burn-out.

Mindfulness and meditation can help you to take the first and necessary step towards recovery, the step that takes you out of your mind, full of restless thoughts and worry about problems and their solutions. This is a very important, but difficult assignment for many people. However, in my experience this is not enough to help you get the true feeling of happiness.

You could describe *Joyfulness* as a logical consequence of Mindfulness. *Joyfulness* lets you experience the flow from a state of 'Being'. The characteristics are movement, pleasure and creativeness, so you don't have to just sit still or concentrate. With *Joyfulness*, you break through the individualism which plays such a major role in the current selfie culture. With *Joyfulness,* you experience the most pleasure by being and creating together. *Joyfulness* takes you to that playful feeling you had as a child. If you can be your true self, and reveal that to others, you can then connect with them. You let them share in your *Joy* and that is so contagious that it can lead to amazing partnerships.

Discover your own Joy and radiate it! Not by looking for it. Not by trying to be someone. You don't perform from *Joyfulness*. Joy has always been inside you, but you lost it somewhere along the way in life. So you can recapture that feeling of Joy by choosing play and self-expression. And by simply being there for others, selflessly.

The joy of discovery is certainly the liveliest

that the mind of man can ever feel

Claude Bernard 1813-1873

The run-up

It's amazing how much can change in just one year! As I write this, it's exactly one year ago since I handed in my notice to my last employer. I had worked as a manager for twenty years, and I'd had enough. I approach everything I do with passion and lots of energy and I noticed that after a difficult period, I had yet again failed to uphold my boundaries. It wasn't a burn-out such as I had experienced in 2006, but I was suffering badly from stress and my body was sending me signals on a daily basis that we couldn't go on like that. I had stuck around for too long in that job, basically for the financial security. My parents raised me to understand that I had to organise my finances properly. That was logical, because they themselves had experienced a time of poverty. Fortunately, they overcame that and were able to send their children to further education. I'm still so grateful to them for that. But I had reached a point where I had to leave that advice behind me and focus on my own happiness. It was a nerve-racking step. Physically, I had too little energy and I clearly felt afraid of change, but I had to do it. In the first instance, it was a matter of sorting things out and laying a new foundation. That meant that I also wanted to establish a normal daily rhythm, despite my exhaustion. Luckily, I already had a healthy diet and lifestyle. How could I not? Margreeth, my wife, is a nutritionist and enjoys preparing delicious and healthy meals every day.

Regular meditation helped me get rid of any tension I had accumulated. That was quite tough going at the beginning. As soon as I was sitting quietly, my legs would start trembling uncontrollably. It was a kind of release that I couldn't stop. That lasted for a week or two. After that, the tension was gone. I read later that animals always do that if they have just been in mortal danger. It releases stress. I suppose you might say I'm a bit slower than an animal.

I really enjoyed doing physical labour in that period. I had to dig ditches for the installation of new pipes and came up with the idea of creating a sheltered spot next to the outdoor sauna. To do so, I had to get a hundred wooden poles into the ground. So I got to work with the manual earth auger and then hammered the poles in. This helped me make a fresh start, escape from my hectic pattern of thinking and free my mind.

It was the ideal moment to take new steps. I found it all very exciting. I'd already made some important choices in my life after the burn-out I'd had in 2006. I was able to elaborate on some of the changes I had initiated back then. In 2016, Margreeth and I had bought an old dike house in Welsum. We didn't know exactly how we were going to renovate it or what we were going to do. We had already started on the renovation when a friend came to stay with us for a while, because of circumstances in her private life. That gave us the idea of building an apartment in the old cellars and bakery. Our friend could then rent it and live there permanently. The renovation was finished quickly, but the situation changed unexpectedly, and the rental didn't happen. There you are, with a beautiful apartment, after an expensive renovation. So we advertised it on Airbnb. It's such a success in Amsterdam, why shouldn't it work out in Welsum? Welsum has so much more to offer! Luckily, we weren't the only ones who thought that way and renting it out was a success, and so quickly, that we made a business of it. It started with the renovation of the apartment and then the arrival of a Lapland Kota. The latter was the result of a wholly intuitive process. I was walking back to the house from the donkey's stable when I saw a hexagonal building in my mind's eye. I had no idea what it was. The first time this happened, I thought no more about it. But two months later, exactly the same thing happened again, at an unexpected moment. I 'saw' it standing there, on the same spot. It was a spot where only a bit of grass was growing. I decided to search Google for hexagonal outbuildings and found out about the Lapland Kota. In Lapland, they also call it a Fire-hut. Margreeth says it's a gnome's house. We soon found a supplier of kotas and a month later it was erected, and already in use. That wasn't ever a goal, it just happened quite intuitively.

Two and a half years later, we discovered a fantastic antique Indian arched façade, and we thought it would be a good idea to build a new home with the ambiance of 1001 Nights. I became completely absorbed in a creative process. Without having made any conscious decision beforehand, and without a plan, a small-scale paradise was finished in only two years. It's a place for wellness, where you can de-stress, have fun and work on your personal development. We call this little paradise '*Andere Wereld*' (Different World) and that's exactly what it is, as you can see on the image below.

Apparently, things work differently here than they do in the 'ordinary world'. Many visitors say that they leave completely changed, without knowing precisely how that happened. Is this the enchanting power of *Andere Wereld*?

Strangely enough, I wasn't really aware of how special this creative process and the end result actually were. I hadn't gone about it in a methodical way. The voice in my head was still active. What now? What else could I do to earn a living? That was the question that kept popping into my head. I had become more intuitive in recent years, but apparently all the stress had pushed it to the background. I had been taught rational deliberation and a methodical future-oriented approach and it was ingrained in me. I had spent more than twenty years in survival mode. My busy job as a manager which demanded I perform well and the fact that one of my children had to be taken into care with serious psychiatric problems had all taken their toll on me. Since I needed to survive, I switched off my feelings. I tried desperately to maintain control from my mind. I could always trust that, couldn't I? My intelligence had got me a long way in my life, hadn't it? There was a good reason why I had done my best to gain a university degree.

The pattern of rational thinking was so ingrained that I didn't even see all we had managed to achieve, naturally, in our business. It was as though all those coincidences and intuitive ideas were irrelevant. For me, they were isolated incidents and I did not connect them to the possibility of looking at things differently. My own conditioning meant I was unable to see another pattern. You only see what you want to see. Or rather, you see only what you're used to seeing. That which fits into your way of thinking. That image of the kota apparently indicated that my field of vision was broadening. And yet it took a very special incident to really turn the tide. It was just before Christmas 2018.

In the spring of that year, I still hadn't gained the insight that a great many things arise from pleasure, play and creation. That ideas come of their own accord without me having to think about them. In fact, that an idea can arise from a vision. I had actually already experienced this with the kota, but apparently it had not sunk in. Margreeth had already told me about her own experiences and had shown me how this worked. I understood it but I didn't feel it and as an approach, it seemed too easy to me. You have to do your best in order to achieve something, don't you? Otherwise it doesn't count as an achievement, right?

For example, I had spent a long time thinking about constructing a garden in the large pasture. I felt it should be the view from the holiday home. In preparation, I had calculated measurements for the garden, drawn plans and worked out how much money I would need to construct it. It was quite a lot of money and I didn't know how I was going to raise it. So I decided to finish the house first, and then we would see. Until the time I wandered into the pasture to feed the donkeys and saw the big pile of old stones in one of the corners. They'd been lying there for a long time and I had already worked out the best way of removing them. However, the high landfill costs stopped me from actually doing so. Apparently, something had already changed in me; suddenly I no longer saw the pile of stones just as a pile of waste. I grabbed a wheelbarrow and started shifting the stones and creating little walls, based only on my intuition. No drawings and no design. I did it purely from the inspiration that arose in that moment. It became a place for meditation. In just one morning, the garden got a completely different appearance and it didn't cost me a penny. By the time I went indoors to have lunch, I was as happy as a child. An intense happiness such as I hadn't felt in a very long time. It was because I had created something based on my feelings. As soon as she saw me, Margreeth asked what was going on. I now know that I was radiating *Joy*. Passers-by think the garden is special. Some visitors say that you can feel that it was made with love. Others ask if it's a place of power. And yes, it is. It's my 'power-from-within place'. And it apparently touches others too.

That morning lugging stones made it instantly clear to me that feelings make inspiration flow, which is when you become creative. Thinking and analysing only get in the way of this creative surge. Creation arises from *Joy* and surrender. This is stating the obvious for an artist, but for a former manager it's a huge step. My feeling of inner joy was awakened by something really simple. My 'Flame of Joy' ignited just because I started piling up stones without any clear plan.

Andere Wereld, Welsum, Netherlands

Illustration: Rob Otterspeer, Epe

The hurdle

I met Margreeth seven years ago, during an Intuitive Development workshop. Margreeth has had health problems since birth. She wasn't expected to live more than a few days. But she did. The life expectancy was changed to a few years and her parents were told she would never walk. Margreeth clearly had other ideas. She started walking and built a normal life for herself.

Mind you... normal? She never lost her playfulness and intuition and those characteristics have taken her a long way. She probably enjoys life so enormously because she has been through so much since she was just a child. Strangely enough, all that has actually given her self-confidence, presumably due to a great mixture of character and upbringing. She is grateful for every day and refuses to feel like a victim, nor will she ever behave as one. Physically, she has many conditional restrictions, but she loves life.

Last year, I asked Margreeth what she would like for her birthday. Her answer was simple: a swing. Her reasons were clear: she wants to play, to go with the rhythm of the swing by setting it in motion herself. A push from someone else is nice, sometimes you need to be pushed. And she lets everyone else play on her swing. Be honest, who doesn't want a swing? She got her swing, attached to a broad bough in the walnut tree. The nice thing is that our guests use it a lot too. Sometimes, there's even a queue of people waiting. Adults love sitting on a swing too! Now and then, you hear someone say what a pity it is that there are no playgrounds for adults.

Margreeth's story, her lust for life and her *Joy* have shown me that much is possible if you are playful and have the confidence to dare to live. It doesn't matter what happened long ago. It doesn't matter how miserable your circumstances are or how low you're feeling at present. Life has so much beauty to offer. But you have to believe in it and want to make it work.

For an illustration of this, look at films of Nick Vujicic on YouTube. He was born without arms and legs, but he travels around the world telling his story. He talks about how every human being is unique, how you have to know what your personal goal in life is, how it's wrong for other people to say that you can't, or could never, do something and that it's nonsense to say that you're worthless.

Okay, so some not so pleasant things happen in your life. That's true for everyone. But your own thoughts are what determine how you feel about things. You have control of that. How do you want to feel? Dejected or lively? Which will you choose?

Yes, which choice will I make? Do I believe in an alternative way of life and do I dare to take an inner decision about that? Or do I say that, but actually hope to continue in the old, trusted manner. I mean, that already got me a long way. Which thoughts about painful events in my life are preventing me from making my own choices? Which thoughts are still forming a hurdle?

I was lucky enough to meet a good coach last year. She helped me get a clear picture of these questions. Of course, I had to find the answers myself. And I did. This time, however, I did have to learn to feel the pain of events from the past. My survival strategy had further repressed my feelings and certainly also my grief. It was soon clear that I would have to take this first hurdle before I could move on.

That hurdle brought me straight back to events in 2006. I had experienced a number of tough events in my private life. I had been extremely busy at work, had not set any boundaries and to top it all, the summer holiday was a disaster. I was only back at work for a few days when I just snapped. I was burnt out. I had pushed myself too hard for years. My energy was gone, and my stress levels were chronically elevated. I lost all sorts of things: my feelings, my enjoyment, my self-confidence, my friends and my hobbies.

I had only been home sick for a week when our child, K, came home for the long-term. Mandatory. K has a psychiatric disorder and against all expectations, turned out to be incapable of following education at a new school. The situation in the family became increasingly worrying and finally, after a few months, K was admitted to a psychiatric institution. It was an incredibly sad and difficult time.

But my burn-out also turned out to have a positive side to it. I re-discovered my unique qualities. My innate talent for being able to sense people and to give energy through my hands. I had pushed this talent to one side twenty years earlier, in order to make a career for myself. But during the time of the burn-out, I had no choice. I felt in everything that I would only become more ill if I tried to carry on living my life unchanged. So, I started a higher professional education programme, to train as an Energy Therapist. That way, I could reinforce my innate talent with knowledge. Having graduated, I started up my own naturopathic practice, where I worked part-time as a therapist. The rest of the time, I did my usual work.

Although I managed to reconstruct some of my inner self in the years following the burn-out, external circumstances did not help. My life started to look more and more like pure survival. I looked for peace among all the hassle, by meditating. I no longer laughed or had fun. At home, I closed myself off from all contact. I was sunk deep in my own thoughts and I was still exhausted. The only strength I felt was the willpower to survive, to be there for our child, living on the edge of the abyss, and our two younger children.

Let me tell you about a few of the things we experienced in that period, and which strained us to our limits. I write 'our' consciously, since that time was also tough on both my wife at the time and our two younger children.

We went through another very hectic period. K caused so much commotion that she was discharged from the institution. And it was such a lovely place. I had spent a week of my holiday decorating and furnishing K's room. But now, she had to move back home with all her things. K had only just arrived home in the afternoon, when she disappeared on her bike. I searched the whole area by bike and car that evening, but she was nowhere to be found. We had called the police, and my ex-wife was at home talking to them. Later that night, the police launched a massive search in the woods. The next morning, a police helicopter was flying over our house, just as our other children were setting off for school on their bikes. Not much later, a forest ranger found K in the woods. Amazingly, she was unharmed. Not that we got a chance to rest; three hours later, we had to take K to the crisis shelter again.

The problems continued at the new location. K ran away again and this time she came back saying she had been sexually assaulted. When I went to report this, I was told that I had to make an appointment to do so and that the vice police had a waiting list of three months. I couldn't believe it, it felt like a slap in the face.

Shortly after, K ran away again and this time, she stole two small articles of clothing from a shop. The weather was bad, and she had left without a coat. It was the first time she had done anything like that. Suddenly, the police did find time for us. The whole thing was blown up out of all proportion. We had to find a lawyer. And all this because a child with a psychiatric disorder had stolen stuff worth 30 euros.

A week after the shoplifting incident, K disappeared from the institution again. Since no-one else did, I went looking for her for the umpteenth time. I wanted to prevent any more hassle; another theft or more abuse. I left photos of K in shops, with my mobile number.

Those were intense years and they had a huge impact. My stress took on impossible proportions. The periods of tranquillity between the incidents were never longer than a couple of days. If my mobile phone rang, adrenaline immediately coursed through my body. For that reason, I never gave others my mobile number. I didn't want any unnecessary stress. The tension you feel if your child is missing, and that child is suicidal too, is almost unbearable. You never get used to it. I was on an emotional roller coaster. You're sad and desperate because it's the umpteenth time that the situation has got out of hand. You love your child, and you want to support them. But that costs you an enormous amount of effort. You try your best to lead a normal life and focus on the other children too. And you get so frustrated by the failure of organisations and institutions. I felt a mixture of grief, anxiety and hope every single day. In addition, we had to try to stay calm, because as the parents, we had an awful lot to sort out with authorities such as the police, the childcare system, child protection and institutions.

And of course, another not entirely unimportant point: we had to work. My ex-wife had a challenging job which demanded she be alert. I was manager of a large department where there was naturally always lots to do. I am therefore an expert when it comes to stress, burn-out, work pressure and pleasure in work. I could add 'unfortunately', but I won't. Because all these intense experiences mobilised me and changed my life for the better. I made a shift from intellect to feelings, from thinking I knew everything to opening up to my innate intuition, from extreme stress to relaxation, from staying in control to letting things just happen and from being result-oriented to being people-oriented. Obviously, this did not happen of its own accord, but there comes a point when you come up against the boundaries of what you can cope with. Even if you resist it. So something had to break inside me first.

That happened early one beautiful morning out on the heath. I had seen Ted Neeley on television a few months earlier. He sang *Gethsemane* from *Jesus Christ Superstar*. The performance had been recorded in New York, in 2006. The singer interprets the song with a wonderful combination of passion, emotion and at the same time, a rawness. Every word, and every phrase touches me deeply. I was leaning against a solitary old tree when the song came to me again, completely unexpectedly, and I shouted it out, deeply affected, in my own way.

I only want to say
If there is a way
Take this cup away from me
For I don't want to taste its poison
Feel it burn me, I have changed

I'm not as sure, as when we started
Then, I was inspired
Now, I'm sad and tired
Listen, surely I've exceeded expectations
Tried for three years, seems like thirty
Could you ask as much from any other man?

God, thy will is hard

But you hold every card

I will drink your cup of poison ...

From that moment, I changed the way I led my life. The 110% of my energy that I was giving was apparently not enough to improve K's situation or my own. How much longer could I continue to ask the impossible of myself without it destroying me? I couldn't cope any longer and realised that I was going to have to leave a large part of the responsibility in this situation to the professionals at the institution. It went against the grain.

During coaching sessions in 2018, I discovered that, seven years later, I was still grieving about that period. I realised just how much responsibility I had shouldered for years and that I had ignored my own boundaries for a long time. That realisation gave me space to make a new start. I turned things around, starting to trust myself and left my anxiety behind me. I banged both fists on the table, to emphasise this. There was no going back!

From that moment on, I stood much more securely on my own two feet. I felt *Joy* from within and the creative juices began to flow.

I had made my decision!

The Joy of discovery

After I had made my decision, I began to trust more and more in the idea that something beautiful could grow from that feeling of *Joy*. That I could achieve something wonderful. Because I had rediscovered my feeling of *Joy*, I also felt the need to keep it to myself. After all the years of stress having the upper hand, I enjoyed this feeling of inner peace which enveloped me like a warm blanket. There was a constant stream of guests coming and going in our holiday homes all through that sunny summer. We enjoyed it. We had some beautiful encounters. It felt as though I were on a journey of discovery on my own property. I felt rich. I woke up every morning with songs in my head. I wanted to hold on to this feeling and it made me want more of it. As a result, the idea of setting up a Spiritual Wellness Arrangement was born. We developed a programme lasting several days and comprising of relaxation in the sauna and in the kota, and a choice of coaching and consulting options. I was still so enthusiastic about what coaching had done for me that I even wanted to start working as a coach. That would allow me to offer our guests even more options in the future. I had a vision of our business in Welsum becoming a refuge. A peaceful spot for people who had lost themselves because they had been under pressure for too long, thanks to the demands of our competitive society. I was so enthusiastic that I registered for two courses at the same time. One was 'Intuitive Coaching'. I chose it because just reading the course contents made me emotional. The other one was focused on stress and burn-out.

So that was it then. I knew what I wanted to do. Now I could start living and also earn my living doing it! What could be nicer than guiding, treating and coaching people in our own retreat centre? It was all I needed. At least, that's what I thought at the time. But I've since learned that you can't just stop a journey of discovery. You never know what's going to happen!

That summer, Margreeth felt the need to give her own feeling of *Joy* an extra impulse. She had just come through a nasty experience with a friend and wanted nothing more than to have a good laugh. She got on the computer and came across a site offering training to become a Laughter Yoga Leader. It was at weekends. She asked if I would go with her. She didn't have to ask me twice. I was immediately on board. Especially when I saw that the training was to be held in Ghent in Belgium. We had always wanted to visit that beautiful medieval Flemish city.

So there we were, early September, in Ghent with beautiful weather. We did laughter exercises in the park. On the second day, I went completely mad. I put on a silly cap and threw my inhibitions to the wind. Margreeth no longer recognised me. The serious man was gone. During those days in Ghent, I was bubbling with energy, all day and evening too. Creative ideas popped into my head, one after the other, effortlessly. It's amazing what having fun and behaving playfully can do for you. I was absolutely gobsmacked. I was living completely IN THE MOMENT, and without meditation or exercises to help direct the focus towards my inner self. So apparently, I could achieve that in other ways, such as by laughing playfully. It was an eye-opener. Within a month, we were giving our own first laughter workshop during a corporate outing. And it was followed by more. I saw that you can build up an awful lot of *Joy* energy as a group; much more than you can on your own, because laughter is infectious. I had honestly never thought about that before. I had experienced the power of *Together*.

After the workshops, and in that autumn, Margreeth and I talked a lot about laughing. At first sight, it seems to be just a superficial, happy occurrence, no more and no less. But we gradually realised that precisely that playfulness and using your intuition enables you to live IN THE MOMENT and create something beautiful along the way. That's why we felt that *Joy* was so important, just as the power of *Together*. We decided to register *Joyfulness* as a trademark and use it as a starting point in coaching and workshops.

Naturally, we were aware of the rise of Mindfulness, which is a method to help you live IN THE MOMENT. In the same way, *Joyfulness* is about the here and now, but it's also about being playful. *Joy* is the source, not the mind. And the great thing is that you can be IN THE MOMENT simply by being free and uninhibited and doing fun things. Being IN THE MOMENT doesn't have to be a difficult task for which you have to practise for a really long time. Another important difference is that *Joyfulness* is reinforced by the power of *Together*.

I made huge strides in my personal development that autumn. My perfectionism disappeared. I dared to try out something new and show it to others. I'm able to trust my intuition more and more in my role as coach. It's becoming stronger. I increasingly feel a mutual connection with the other person. I receive indications for the coaching because I see images and symbols which have to do with the feelings and past history of the coachee. This helps me better understand why the coachee has blocked their emotions and it makes the talks we have more intense.

That December, I experienced something which turned out to be crucial for me.

It was just before Christmas, and a couple had recently stayed with us who were having a lot of problems with their nine-year-old son. They had just been through a really rough period and this was the first time they had taken a break together in a long time. The man was deeply troubled by feelings of guilt. Their story was very similar to my experiences with K. I told them how it had all affected me and how I had dealt with the situation. We had wonderful talks with each other, in which we shared many experiences and fortunately, laughed heartily together too.

A couple of days before Christmas, I drove to a shop two hours away to buy wood strips. I got chatting to the saleswoman and guess what? The man who had been our guest and with whom I had spoken, used to live above that shop and still worked for that company. I was taken completely by surprise. She told me that he was at that moment working at one of the company's other locations. I decided to go and visit him. I actually had another appointment that afternoon, but this was so special, I felt I just had to go. The road I took went along the dike for a while, then I had to take a ferry across the river and drive along the dike on the other side. I managed to find the workplace and I saw him bent over a table made of a tree trunk, working. He didn't see me until I was about a metre away. He looked up, surprised. He told me that he thought daily about my words and that they were still helping him with his feelings of guilt. He had woven a coloured thread through his watch strap as a tangible reminder. I was very moved; I had no idea I'd had this effect on him. He then asked me how I had travelled there. I told him and he asked to see my car.

Naturally, I didn't understand why. After he had looked at the car, he asked me to drive home by way of the shop I had just visited, because he would like to give me a present, as a token of his gratitude. He had been thinking about it for some time but didn't know how to get it to me. He phoned the shop to tell them to expect me and to give me something. We said a fond farewell and I drove back to the shop along the dike and on the ferry. A huge wooden sculpture was waiting there for me. It was a beautiful head, carved in a large, weathered tree trunk. I couldn't believe my eyes. I suddenly understood the question about the car, since the sculpture only just fitted into it. The event overwhelmed me and made me emotional and when I got home, I sent him a message. He told me that the title of the sculpture was 'Aryan', which means 'The Noble One'.

I had never been able to appreciate the meaning of coincidences and intuitive ideas because I was so rational. But this event had such an impact that I was unable to sleep the whole night; so much energy was released in me. It was a wonder, and a sign that from that moment on, I could have complete faith in life.

The discovery of Joy

A new year has begun. So much happened in the second half of 2018 that I can't wait to see what 2019 will bring. In recent weeks, I've been told a few times that I have to open up a bit more; that I can mean something to others and that it's a shame to inhibit myself. Margreeth is convinced that I'm going to write a book. She had got this in December from my deceased father. The two of them still have a very good connection. Apparently, he indicated that the book would be finished by May. It's now mid-January and I have absolutely no inclination to put pen to paper, never mind that this book could be finished by May. It would seem I still have trouble listening to what my father says.

In January, the coach training deals with the theme Inner Child. During a meditation on this, I see myself as a six-year-old boy in the school playground. I have to stand with both feet neatly between the lines of a paving stone, otherwise I will be punished, and if I misbehave, the whole class will be punished. I don't want that to happen.

I describe that image to a fellow student. Obviously, it's clear that as a child, I learned to stay neatly within the lines; lines that others had drawn for me. In agreement with my fellow student, I write this message on a piece of paper and stand on it. Immediately, a long-lasting and cramp-like pain shoots through my left leg. I can feel it all the way to in my hip. The thing is, I have regularly had problems with my left leg and foot since I left my job, but the pain is unbearable now. I take a new piece of paper and write: 'I walk my own path'. At first, I was going to write FOLLOW, but I scored that out straight away. What do you mean, follow? I'm never following anyone ever again! From now on, I'm going to walk my own path. When I stand on the new text, the pain and cramp fade within a few seconds. That deep-rooted message came back after more than fifty years and I can replace it with a new one. Since that day, it feels as though the brakes have been released. I feel freer in everything I do.

A week later, I go to London with Margreeth. We've registered for a five-day Laughter Yoga Teacher training course. If we gain the certificate, we will be able to train Leaders ourselves. I become more and more fascinated by laughter, so much so that I get other people laughing increasingly easily, and they have the same effect on me. I notice it in another area too. I get inspired by the stories the other participants tell, and by the things they are planning to do. I note that they dare to think big. Why don't I? Or do I not want to? What's going on with me? Am I keeping myself small because I don't dare, or am I keeping myself small because I find life together in our Welsum dike house enough? I experience the power of *Together* even more strongly than during the first training.

Back home, I immediately talk to my coach. We agree that I will write a text for my website about the mission and vision I have for my Joyfulness coaching. The next day, the first letters are on my screen. I think two A4 pages will be more than enough. At the end of the day, I have written fifteen pages and I'm still not finished. The next day there are 27, and I've still got so much more to tell. This goes on for a couple of days. By the end of the week, I'm suddenly talking about 'my book'. Margreeth has a great laugh at my expense about it. I'm talking about the book I never intended to write. How amazing is this?

In the next three weeks, I write another 120 pages. Now it really is a book. My original idea was just to note my vision on coaching, but as I wrote, it went much further. It's become a book which takes a critical look at the current choices in society and the opportunities there are for living and working together in another way. In addition to being a personal document, it's also a call to look at things differently, work in another way and approach our children differently. So it goes a lot further than just a vision on coaching. I'm wondering what I can do with this book. How big do I want to make this? And while I'm wondering this more and more often, I have a dream.

I see a three-dimensional symbol in a dark space. It's electrically charged and emitting a pulsating white light. It approaches me slowly and penetrates my forehead. I see a bare trunk growing out of the earth; the top takes a few turns and grows back into the ground, next to the original trunk.

The whole trunk is covered with all sorts of flowers, in a variety of colours. I see roses, carnations and irises, to name but a few. From two buds, birds are growing. I think it's strange, and it looks weird. I want to touch a bird and precisely as my hand touches the feathers, I hear classical Indian music. Music that touches me deeply and makes me curious about the other bird. As soon as I touch it, I hear a woman's voice singing a mantra. This is such a special plant; I really want one. I read the name on a sticker: 'Ananda'.

I've heard of the name before. Some oriental shops and yoga studios have that name. But not knowing much about the terminology of Indian philosophy, I have no idea what the name means. I look it up the next morning and find the following quote: "The Ananda which is the source of our being, is the source of our pleasure or Joyfulness." I couldn't believe it!

This dream heralds the beginning of yet another new phase. Completely independently, Margreeth and I get the feeling that we need to promote *Joyfulness*. We both see that there are social problems, and *Joyfulness* could well be the solution to the performance society with its constant competition. We secure the domain name joyfulness.world. During a course I take, in March, I talk to others about our plans. About how I want to do things differently and not think small anymore. We do a kind of game in the break and I pick a card from a set. It says 'fearless'. In the book that goes with it, I read: 'This is not the time to take small, hesitant steps. This is the time to make a grand gesture, grasp the opportunity and be courageous.' That's good enough for me. I have experienced the power of *Together* many times recently. Now is the time to use that power, to put an end to the time of being alone. We're going to set up a collaborative partnership with independent entrepreneurs who want to spread the mission of *Joyfulness*: *The Joyfulness Cooperative.* We want to set aside a part of the profits to support *Joyful* goals worldwide. We soon realise that a lot of people are responding enthusiastically. They think it's a great idea and an inspiring story.

Many of them want to support our mission, but not all of them are entrepreneurs. Which means they can't become members of an entrepreneurs' cooperative. What now? The answer comes to me as I'm crawling behind a van in traffic. Written on the van is: Friends of the Dike House. Being the owner of our dike house, I take that as a sign. I'm becoming more and more sensitive to such signs. I look up the name on the Internet and see that it belongs to a foundation which has an idealistic goal that the Friends support. That's what we need. So, in addition to the cooperative, we set up the Friends of Joyfulness Foundation. That way, we reach everyone, and even more people can support the projects.

So that's the situation now. One year ago, I emerged from a difficult period, went travelling, and completed my fascinating 'Journey of discovery'. Through my experiences along the way, it turned out that I had made my very own 'Discovery of Joy'. What a thrilling journey of discovery it was. I wish everyone could experience it. In fact, I wish all of us such a 'together' journey. I started this part of the book with a quote from Claude Bernard: "The joy of discovery is certainly the liveliest that the mind of man can ever feel." I personally didn't discover a new world, but a different one. A world of *Joy*. "The discovery of Joy is certainly the liveliest that the mind of man can ever feel".

Being Joyful is our natural state of being

Deepak Chopra

Joyfulness

How can you experience your *Joy*? Or do you already experience your *Joy*, but you'd like to know more about it? What is needed to feel it and how does it work? What exactly is that *Joyfulness* feeling? It's high time we got that clear.

The best way to describe *Joyfulness* is as a strong feeling of inner happiness. *Joy* lies deep inside you. It's power and happiness at the same time. It feels as though fire and light are burning in your stomach. It's the champagne bubbles you feel sparkling deep inside you. At the same time, it's a source of peace, of being totally yourself. You feel that peace because you're connected to others and don't feel the need to meet all sorts of demands and expectations. *Joy* is nourished by the soul. In that sense, you might define *Joy* as 'happiness coming from the soul'. It's a blissful state of 'Being' that comes from the heart.

There's a good reason why *Joyfulness* is called 'the natural state of being' in Buddhism. The natural state of 'Being' that remains once you have shaken off all the commotion and mental stress.

The feeling of *Joy* is present in the HERE AND NOW. You can't hold on to it. You feel that happiness if you let your heart speak and if you feel genuinely connected to people or animals. Other people see and feel that. They also see your *Joy* when you make or do beautiful things, and that inspires them. It's a synergy, because *Joy* is not only in you. Nor is it a skill you can teach yourself and train. *Joy* arises inside you through synergy with others. You give and receive *Joy* simultaneously. You radiate *Joy*, from the inside out. It feels good to be able to light the fire within yourself and let it burn. You can warm up and light everything around you that way. You beam your *Joy*. Do you know of any fire that doesn't warm and light the environment? Any fire that doesn't do that isn't much use. The degree to which you connect to the world around you determines the degree of *Joy*.

I always feel *Joy* when I'm giving people healing or talking with people. I feel compassion rising in me and the energy starts to flow. It makes no difference how I'm feeling in myself. Even when I'm out of sorts, when I connect with others from my heart, I feel *Joy*. I sometimes even feel better in myself afterwards. Even in difficult times, and under difficult circumstances, you can get energy from your *Joy*. You can be sad, and at the same time *Joyful*.

Does that sound strange? Do you think that's impossible? I can understand that, since most people confuse *Joyfulness* with Happiness. However, there is a great difference between the two. Happiness is feeling joyous because of external circumstances. You got your driving licence, for example, or you've just had a lovely dinner with friends or one of your children has come home from a trip around the world. You feel 'happy' as a result of events and activities that are short-lived. It's gone before you realise it. Not that that makes it any less pleasing. And do enjoy it while it lasts! But *Joyfulness,* on the other hand, is not dependent on such things. *Joy* occurs when you are genuinely 'Being', a 'Being' that feels connected to a greater whole. And if that's your basic feeling, you will have little or no need of short-lived peaks of happiness.

Joyfulness awakens when you realise that there is a unique personal power inside you, and when you embrace your authentic self. That gives so much bliss. You are filled with pleasure and you feel calm, energetic and powerful. This is the real you, in the HERE AND NOW. By being yourself, you can connect to others in a natural way. You can reveal yourself as the person you are.

It's wonderful to experience that feeling of *Joy*. You radiate it, and other people find it catching. It's a radiance, and one of its meanings is: 'showing great *Joy*'. It's shine, brilliance and beauty; all names for the radiation of your *Joy*. It's a radiance that you won't get from fillers and injectables. They can't compete.

And you can change your surroundings with your radiance. *Joy* always touches everyone; it's catching. It helps you meet people whom you inspire, and who in turn inspire you. You are stimulated to grow further, and others are stimulated to develop further. I've had many of these encounters in the last year, one after the other. The most special one for me was of course the meeting I described in the story about 'Aryan'. But there were other encounters which were equally worthwhile.

You can show *Joy* in many different ways. One important way is through self-expression and creativity. You can take up something creative that suits your talent and passion; making music, dancing, painting, telling stories. Light-hearted or not. And it certainly doesn't have to be grandiloquent. For example, you can get together with a group of people and cook an extensive meal or help a group of friends with their renovation. Or in my case, start up a cooperative with a group of entrepreneurs in order to be able to convey a mission. Whatever it is, if you do it together, huge strength is released and you can have a whole lot of fun together.

> ### A joy shared is a joy doubled

You can also radiate *Joy* without it necessarily leading to something concrete. You can just be there for others because you are engaged, and you need nothing in return. You connect to others from your heart. Not for any personal gain, but because you want to do something for others. You might, for example, go for a walk with someone who is lonely. This will definitely multiply the feeling of *Joy*. Simply 'Being' there for others more than pays itself back, even though that was never your intention. It will surprise you time and again just how much energy this generates. You see this in neighbourliness, when neighbours help and support each other. I didn't know that word, being a city dweller. So I was taken aback when our neighbour offered to mow the grass on our side of the dike when we'd only just come to live in Welsum. He pushed his small lawnmower back and forth the whole afternoon in the heat of the sun. I wondered in amazement what kind of world I had landed in. It was indeed a different one.

So you can make a difference with your own creation, by being there for someone in need, by working out an innovative idea, by starting up a new social initiative, by helping someone or by making art. There are many ways to make a difference, and most importantly you shouldn't let yourself be restricted in expressing *Joy*. It's a very personal thing, and that makes it quite unique.

You can only really connect to others if you don't judge and are not biased. A first step is recognising that you are prejudiced. It's unavoidable. Everyone is prejudiced, so be aware of it. You only know a small part of the other person and in addition, you often look through glasses which are coloured by your own background, culture and religion. It seems a difficult thing to change, but you can work on it. I have personal experience of this. This was an important learning point during my training as a therapist because - and I can't say this often enough - you cannot have a compassionate contact with another person if you think beforehand that you know what they are like. Bias always gets in the way of *Joy* and genuine contact. It puts a screen between you and the other person.

You will achieve a deeper, more intense contact if you use your intuition. That makes you more receptive to them. You open up. Intuition has a strong surprise element, in fact. You suddenly get new insights and see new possibilities ahead. With intuition, worthwhile, creative ideas spring spontaneously to mind, and you learn things about the other person. And all this is effortless. The ideas come to you without you understanding where they come from. Whether you design, heal someone or you are coaching;

whether you compose music, cook or are engaged in conversation; whether you write or paint, an awful lot happens in this process. You're having to deal with emotions, motivation, inspiration, imagination, impulses and intuition. My innate intuition has been put under pressure during my life by my enormous need for control. That tendency returns at moments when I don't dare to trust my feeling and my intuition. I fall back on my rational thinking.

After all the life events, training and insights, I have experienced several wonderful intuitive moments in the last year, while carrying out healing or while coaching. My fear of feeling has lessened. I notice that in particular because I have become more and more receptive to images. For example, I once saw a huge orange pumpkin lying on the table. Shortly afterwards, it turned out that the pumpkin evoked memories of an intense and emotional family event during childhood. And then there was the colourful little umbrella in the ice cream. That signified the vulnerable relationship with the mother; the daughter always broke the umbrella sticks in two. And so on. There are countless examples. When I shared this information with the coachees, it released deep-seated emotions in them. And that allowed them to move forward in their personal process. These are gifts which make me feel really *Joyful*.

Rational thinking plays a subordinate role in this whole process of *Joyfulness*. You don't think up a goal beforehand. The most amazing ideas and information just occur. Of their own accord. Research confirms that you make hardly any use of conscious rational thinking while you're doing or making something intuitively. This is consciousness-raising. Artists say that they have entered a different state of 'Being'.

Picasso described how, during the creative process, he went through a number of phases every time. According to him, you first enter the state of fullness, which is followed by the state of emptying. And that repeats itself again and again. He called that the secret of art. I can no longer ask this question of the great artist, naturally, but I wonder what Picasso meant by fullness? I get the impression that *Joyfulness* comes very close to his inner perception. You can see that when you look at his beautiful painting 'The Joy of Life' from 1906. It shows girls of marriageable age dancing and playing the flute.

Carl Rogers (1961), the famous American psychotherapist, says that there are three important characteristics needed for you to express yourself creatively, and you can develop them.

- Be open to experiences

You're free of psychological defence, which means you can let your thoughts and memories flow without judgement, emotional rejection or earlier conditioning. You dare to try out ideas and allow new discoveries.

- Inner strength and self-confidence

You judge yourself and the world, based on your own opinions and emotional responses. The opinions of others are, in fact, unimportant. You create that which is of value to you, not to use to please others.

- An ability to play

Your inner child is still present, you experiment, go exploring and you are capable of play. You allow yourself to picture various possibilities, regardless of whether or not they seem realistic.

You see that this fits perfectly with my description of *Joyfulness*. The ability to play, which goes together with a growing self-confidence and an increasing personal strength, is clearly expressed in Rogers' words. As is the importance of being unbiased and open to the world around you.

> *The intuitive mind is a sacred gift and the rational mind is a faithful servant. We have created a society that honors the servant and has forgotten the gift.*
>
> Albert Einstein

Inspiration

There are wonderful examples to be found of people who have used their passion and personal energy to create and develop something that turned out to be much bigger than they could ever have thought possible. The stories are similar. They came from a unique passion and commitment. What these people created from their *Joy* is magnificent. And that wasn't their original intention.

I can think of two such initiatives in particular which appeal to my imagination and have inspired me enormously.

The first one is the Plastic Whale initiative. While travelling around the world, Marius Smit had seen an incredible amount of plastic floating in the sea. He decided to do something about it. He wanted to build a boat out of the plastic waste in the canals of Amsterdam: The Plastic Whale. It seemed like an impossible plan, but three years later the boat was completed. I was lucky enough to be able to attend a personal presentation by him. Marius was determined to have his plan succeed at any cost, and he spoke so passionately about his dream that he managed to enlist the help of hundreds of people, volunteers and businesses. Ten thousand plastic bottles were fished out of the water and used to build a boat that was six metres long. And that was only the beginning. To me, that's a beautiful example of *Joy*.

Fishing for plastic in Amsterdam with the Plastic Whale Foundation

'Plastic Whale is the first Plastic Fishing Company in the world. A social enterprise with a mission: to make the world's waters plastic-free. We do that by fishing for plastic with as many people as possible. And from the plastic we fish up, we build beautiful design sloops. We currently have a fleet of ten design boats built from Amsterdam Canal plastic and we use the boats to fish for plastic in Amsterdam and Rotterdam.'

www. plasticwhalefoundation.com

The second example is Mick Bröcker. He is a meditation teacher and founder of the Ombir Foundation. He writes books about personal development, meditation and mindfulness.

Mick was still a student when his grandmother died and he left for Tibet for an undetermined period, where he lived in a monastery with Tibetan monks. On his return to the Netherlands, he founded the Ombir Foundation. His mission was to give orphans there a better future. Since late 2015, he has been staying in Nepal, near his orphans. The Ombir Children's Home has since been built and the children attend school. One hundred percent of all donations is used for the education of the boy and girls.

I first heard about him on a Dutch late-night talk show. I saw a young man with a mission sitting there. And it touched me deeply.

On his website, ombir.org, Mick writes: 'I believe that if you want to shine in today's world, you have to give one hundred percent of yourself.' And that's exactly the point. If you give one hundred percent of yourself, you are present in *Joyfulness.* As I said earlier, the 'natural state of being'. Being completely yourself results in what I call 'unique *Joy*'.

"I believe that if you want to shine in today's world, you have to give one hundred percent of yourself.

As long as I can remember, I have believed that I live to give. Live to give. Whatever it is that makes your heart beat faster.

It will always be something that allows you to serve others. Always is and always will be.

Be the change you want to see in the world."

Live to give

"Live to give. Whatever it is that makes your heart beat faster." This is part of the quote by Mick. The great thing about this quote is that if you live to give, it will always be something that allows you to serve others. It needn't be directly visible. The two stories I just highlighted are wonderful, of course, but it need not always be on such a grand scale. Every little contribution based on Joy changes something for the better. However small it may seem.

And here too, it's about just doing things based on who you really are. If you're yourself, you have enormous Joy inside you. And if you radiate that from your heart, you will always make a difference. Simply by being who you are, you touch others. You connect your passion and your dream with your feeling of fervour. That changes everything.

You infect other people with your energy and charisma. It just happens. The Joy in you can be seen and felt by everyone and they all want to hitch a lift on it, subconsciously and sometimes consciously. Try not laughing if you're sitting next to someone who is laughing uncontrollably. It's a good trick if you can resist. At first you try to control yourself, but the energy piles up and at a certain point, you can no longer resist. You burst out laughing too. The fire you have ignited in you gets bigger and bigger and when it's hot enough, it envelops the people around you. Some people respond more quickly than other, but Joy is incredibly infectious.

Live to give. But what is it you're giving? And how do you give it? You give based on your unique being, your unique talent and your unique passion. By being yourself, you make connections and ensure change. Giving is not an accomplishment. If you reveal yourself, it happens of its own accord and without you realising it. You're not thinking about it at all. It's actually giving, without the action of giving. It's giving without wanting anything in return. That makes you feel Joyful.

So it's completely different to giving something and expecting something in return. If you do that, you're actually seeking approval and validation. You want to be seen and appreciated. You're giving with 'quid pro quo' at the back of your mind and that makes giving a conscious act. A great many people have been raised with this conviction, but it only forms an obstacle to your happiness. If you just give unconditionally from yourself, you don't need any approval at all from others. And the great thing is that this is exactly when you feel happy. By giving Joy, you get Joy back. It's an exchange.

> *"You give but little when you give of your possessions. It is when you give of yourself that you truly give. There are those who give with joy, and that joy is their reward. And there are those who give with pain, and that pain is their baptism.*
>
> *And there are those who give and know not pain in giving, nor do they seek joy, nor give with mindfulness of virtue; they give as in yonder valley the myrtle breathes its fragrance into space. Through the hands of such as these God speaks, and from behind their eyes He smiles upon the earth.*
>
> *It is well to give when asked, but it is better to give unasked, through understanding."*
>
> Kahlil Gibran

I differentiate between two forms of giving. From *Joy of Sharing*, you reveal yourself. You make contact with others and give them attention and *Joy*. You share your *Joy* with others, and that's wonderful! But with one important addition: you give predominantly from yourself. You give from that which you think is needed.

From *Joy of Compassion*, the contact you make is more emotional and intuitive. You support the other and give them what they really need and not what you think they need. And you don't give only to those you love. That way, you can also be a healer. Giving is also asking the other person what is needed. They themselves know best.

There is an important consideration attached to giving. If you give to someone in order to show what a good person you really are, you're actually taking something from them... self-esteem and equality. It's an illusion to think that this is giving unconditionally.

A recent study by a group including Lynn Alden, professor of psychology at the University of British Columbia in Canada, shows that our personal *Joy* is created by 'bringing out the good in other people through kindness'. She says that we should just be kind to others without inflating our own importance. If we do that spontaneously, without that 'quid pro quo', that will give us the feeling of *Joy*. It doesn't matter how large or how small your contribution is.

She also says that in these times, the majority of people do not respond to this. Sadly, we are strongly influenced by striving to be the best and earn the most money. 'Me, me' is the priority.

The following text caught my attention. It's the outcome of an extensive study into the happiness effect of giving and receiving, published at the end of 2018.

The joy of giving lasts longer than the joy of getting

Date: December 20, 2018 Source: Association for Psychological Science

In two studies, psychology researchers Ed O'Brien (University of Chicago Booth School of Business) and Samantha Kassirer (Northwestern University Kellogg School of Management) found that participants' happiness did not decline, or declined much slowly, if they repeatedly bestowed gifts on others versus repeatedly receiving those same gifts themselves.

The data, from a total of 96 participants, showed a clear pattern: Participants started off with similar levels of self-reported happiness and those who spent money on themselves reported a steady decline in happiness over the 5-day period. But happiness did not seem to fade for those who gave their money to someone else. The joy from giving for the fifth time in a row was just as strong as it was at the start.

They conducted a second experiment online. Again, the self-reported happiness of those who gave their winnings away declined far more slowly than did the happiness reported by those who kept their winnings. Further analyses ruled out some potential alternative explanations, such as the possibility that participants who gave to others had to think longer and harder about what to give, which could promote higher happiness.

Sciencedaily.com

The conclusion was music to my ears: 'The joy of giving lasts longer than the joy of getting.' This wonderful fact has now been proven even scientifically.

Flow

The expression 'being in the flow' has been assimilated into daily language. "I'm nicely in the flow". If you ask people to name an activity which feels comfortable and good, they generally give an example in which they had a feeling of flow.

The term 'flow' was introduced by the American-Hungarian psychologist Mihaly Csikszentmihalyi in 1975. He describes flow as a state of happiness and satisfaction in which you immerse yourself totally during an activity. It feels as if everything is going effortlessly. You are challenged, you have the feeling that you have everything under control, and you are so focused on the activity that you are unaware of yourself or of the time.

Someone who lives by *Joyfulness* will often experience being in the flow if they go to work filled with energy and a deeply rooted pleasure. The resulting flow envelops you without you having consciously thought about it for even a second.

When I think of flow, memories immediately spring to mind. They have to do with circumambulation. Circumambulation is a ritual act of moving around a sacred object or idol. It can be found in almost all major religions: Islam, Christianity, Buddhism, Hinduism, Judaism and Sikhism.

My first such memory is walking around the Bodnath Stupa, one of the largest ancient temples in South Asia. It's in Kathmandu, the capital of Nepal. Buddhists walk a meditative pilgrimage, known as a 'kora', consisting of 108 times around the stupa. After I had walked some rounds, I became completely disoriented by the many twists and turns along the way. I no longer knew who or what I was, I lost all sense of time and was totally immersed in the act of walking.

I had a similar experience walking in a maze. I had the same feeling of disorientation and being immersed in what I was doing. I zigzagged from the centre back to the entrance and felt myself getting increasingly happy. Happier and happier. Once there, it turned out that other people had the same experience.

Incidentally, the feeling of *Joyfulness* clearly goes a step further than just experiencing flow. Flow is what you feel when you are completely immersed in an activity. That can be a solo activity which is not at all *Joyful*. A burglar can be completely in the flow if he manages to strip the whole house within an hour. You experience the feeling of *Joyfulness* if you are doing something for others, from your heart and with *Joy*. You may well experience moments of flow at the same time.

Well-known American psychologist Maslow has shown that in general, people who experience personal growth enjoy life more (Maslow 1999). They respect life, are amazed by it and grateful for it. They are independent-thinking people who are not overly influenced by the prevailing social attitudes. They are not egocentric and have a deeply rooted sense of connectedness to other people. That's the clear similarity to *Joyfulness*.

Incidentally, flow is not only a modern notion, nor is it restricted to our western society. Such experiences were known in ancient times too. Worldwide. You can read about them in old scriptures. Below is a list of some striking descriptions from the past.

Flow in other cultures

Peruvian nature religions describe Kausay Puriy as the ability to live in such a way that energy always flows: 'walking in living energy'. This life force is in everyone and reveals itself through a deep belief in yourself and your fellow humans. It's up to you to tap into that uniqueness in yourself, to develop it and show it to the outside world. Every individual can give themselves a face of their own, but you then have to walk your own path in life. So it's not important how you express yourself, as long as you reach your destiny in life. You can't compare your destiny to that of someone else. It's a gift you can give yourself by trusting in your inner light and inner strength. Let yourself be carried by the waves of Sami, the flow of water in its natural state.

In the *Alchemy of Happiness,* al-Ghazali, a twelfth-century Islamic philosopher, writes that the person who knows themselves knows true happiness. He believes we are all born with pain in our souls because we have forsaken God. That makes us feel constantly unhappy. We try to ease the pain through physical pleasure and enjoyment. But that can never relieve a pain which is essentially spiritual. The only answer to that pain in your soul is to get to know yourself. However, self-knowledge cannot be achieved through rational thinking or philosophy. You will find the ultimate feeling of happiness in music and in dance, such as that of the whirling Dervishes. By turning around and around, you lose any self-consciousness and enter a state of euphoria, a state of flow.

About 2,300 years ago, the Chinese philosopher, Zhuangzi, wrote the first essay on Happiness, entitled *Supreme Happiness.*

Zhuangzi explains that there are two kinds of happiness in Taoism. Most people focus on wealth, fame, comfort and materialism. If that's what you seek, you will become increasingly unhappy if you don't achieve it. The other kind of happiness is Wuwei, which is the art of following Tao, The Way. You might regard this as flow. Wuwei is the art of doing nothing against this flow; in other words, going with the flow, living in the moment.

When you do things from your soul

you feel a river moving in you

a joy

Rumi

Inspiration
Joy of transformation
Joy of compassion
Intuition
Joy of creating
Joy of sharing
Joy
Blaze of Joy
Flame of Joy
Spark of Joy
Fertile soil
Joyless

Inspiration	You're Joyful and have a radiance of Joy in life and work. Your passion is fused with your mission. Inspiration is the light that stimulates being in Joy at all stages.
Intuition	Intuition is the centre in which Joy lives. It protects and supports you. By using your intuition you are in contact with your inner self and others. It stimulates innovation.
Joy of transformation	Working together on a mission (cooperative creating). You are changing the organisation, the community and even the world.
Joy of creating	Your inner Joy is manifestating in the world. You are creating by the expression of passionate energy.
Joy of compassion	Your inner Joy makes an empathic connection with others. You live and work form your heart. You support others in their needs. Not just giving to others for your own sake.
Joy of sharing	Your inner Joy is radiating. You're really connecting with other people and you are showing yourself. You support others as an expression of your needs. You feel confident.
Joy	You can feel your inner Joy. You enjoy life and have a feeling of inner peace. You feel free and playful and you have a connection to your inner self and to others.
Blaze of Joy	You'are still looking for a balance between feelings of Joy and gravity or caution. You're not feeling completely free in connection with yourself and others.
Flame of Joy	You can have short periods of Joy and feelings of pleasure. But you are still vulnerable and in need of support from others to grow. Sometimes there is a twinkle in the eyes.
Spark of Joy	You feel inspired by others who are Joyful. But you don't know in which way you can build your own Joy yet. You have a feeling that a personal development is starting and you are looking for support.
Fertile soil	The importance of a good foundation. Awareness of your body and mind by meditation/ mindfulness, healthy living and finding peace in nature.
Joyless	Below foundation level. You lost touch with your inner self. Low confidence and self-esteem, withdrawn from connections, no pleasure or playfulness. Symptoms of burn-out or depression.

Achieve or maintain Joy?

Naturally, it's wonderful to be *Joyful* in life. You are passionate and driven and in direct contact with your inner *Joy.* You convey the energy you feel within to those around you. That's fantastic. Of course, even in these situations, you have to keep an eye on whether you have enough energy and strength. They fluctuate constantly. Giving one hundred percent of yourself is not, in fact, a fixed thing. You're continually having new experiences and all sorts of things can happen in your life. So *Joy* is not a permanent feeling. It's a process that continually requires energy and adjustment. The art is in keeping the fire burning in a different way every time. It's important to keep an open mind towards your surroundings and take on new challenges.

Sadly, there are incredibly large numbers of people who don't know, or no longer know, that feeling of *Joy.* Unnoticed, they have gradually lost their innate *Joyfulness.* Life events, our upbringing and the opinions and beliefs of others which are embedded in us, are behind this. Education also often plays a negative part in this. At school, we are taught to adhere to social norms. Otherwise, we don't count. That's what makes your unique 'Being' disappear.

How can you evoke that feeling of *Joyfulness*? And who wouldn't want to do that? The unfortunate answer is that there is no standard approach that works for everybody. There are no tricks to help you reach your authentic *Joy.* We are accustomed to the idea of practising and learning if we want to achieve something. That doesn't apply to *Joyfulness.* You actually need to unlearn something; all that behaviour and all those limiting beliefs that you have been taught. They get in the way of feeling *Joy.*

Even when you do things from *Joyfulness,* you come up against personal, spiritual and physical boundaries. This can cause you to lose the feeling of *Joyfulness.* You may be too focused on your goal along the way. You want so badly to be or to achieve something that you look too far ahead. You lose pleasure in doing things and lose touch with yourself and your *Joy.* Stress sets in. You lose sight of your higher goal and with this loss, you also lose your sense of *Joyfulness*.

While all the time, just by 'Being', you will reach the goal. Unnoticed. From *Joy* and the connection with others. That's why it's not a question of 'wanting' nor a question of 'becoming'. It's a question of 'Being'.

"If I think, tomorrow, that I'm going for gold, I will do too much. I'll be standing at the beginning of the 500 metres like a pumped-up Hulk, and that's not the right idea.

I have to skate smoothly and pay attention to my technique. And at the end of the day, I'll see what position I end in. Yes, I realise it's a dozy answer, but it's all you're getting."

Ice skater Kjeld Nuis, 23-2-2019

Joyless

Joyless means that you have lost your inner motivation; you have no energy or determination. You feel down and you're melancholy. However, there's no such thing as 100% Joyless. Whatever the gravity of the situation, I believe that there's always a tiny ray of hope. And that tiny ray can be made to shine more brightly. So Joyless can be a temporary state in which you land, for example if you have been demanding too much of yourself and ignoring your boundaries. That's what happens to you if you have a burn-out.

But Joyless can also be a chronic condition. If so, ask yourself the following questions. What is it I want, actually? How would my life have to be, to make me feel happy? What gives me pleasure? These are difficult questions to answer because you no longer know your own feelings, and no longer know what it is you want most, deep in your heart. That has left you without self-confidence, so you let yourself be guided by what other people think of you. You want to be perfect for them, so you have to constantly be on your toes. That guzzles energy and if you go a long time without getting in touch with your *Joy,* depression is lying in wait.

I meet a lot of people in my practice who have little energy and a lot of tension. They have muscle problems, headaches, back problems, stiff necks, stomach and intestinal problems, insomnia and a host of other ailments. These are often a consequence of overload, biting off more than they can chew. They have to perform. People suffering like this generally realise that they will have to change things in their lives and look for alternative work. However, they don't know what exactly it is that they want or how to achieve that. They have no enjoyment, feel very small and inhibited and carry a feeling of guilt around with them. They are almost always perfectionists with a great sense of responsibility, both at work and outside it. So if something then goes wrong, it has a snowball effect. Their self-confidence diminishes, leaving them less able to cope with criticism which they try to avoid by attempting to do everything even more perfectly. You can be sure that's not going to work out. It's a tense situation in which there is no room for playfulness or putting things into perspective. Consequently, these people dare less and less, stop going out and eventually retreat into themselves.

At the end of 2018, a woman came to my practice with a long list of ailments. She had been tired for months, was suffering from an oppressive feeling in her chest and had difficulty breathing deeply. She also had muscle pains in her neck, shoulders and upper arms, which were very tense. She was worried and was especially concerned that she might have heart problems. She was a patient of a specialist at the hospital. There had been blood tests, an ECG and various other examinations and the hospital had done everything they could to find out what was wrong with her. The results were not yet known, and she didn't want to wait for them. All these ailments were causing her too much suffering. So she came to me, in the hope that my treatment would reduce them. She had heard good things about me and so was willing to try this. Her family and friends advised her against it because they are all sceptical about all that alternative stuff in naturopathy.

Nevertheless, to her own utter amazement, she was able to relax deeply during the first session and after the second session a couple of days later, she was her old self again. The breathlessness and tension were gone, and she had much more energy. The hospital test results later showed no signs of physical problems, everything was fine, luckily. When we got talking, it turned out that she had other problems. Things were not going well at work, she felt trapped and would have liked to do something she was good at. But she didn't dare to broach the subject with her boss, believing it would have no effect. And that was spoiling her pleasure in life at that time.

I can give you many more examples of people I have treated for similar ailments in these last years. They became ill due to long-term exposure to stress. One of the causes of that stress was they didn't dare to or couldn't be themselves. At a certain point, that will come back on you and physical problems will develop. This all costs a fortune in medicines, doctors' visits and hospital expenses while there's often a very personal and sad story hidden behind those problems.

You have to want to listen to that story, and you can only do that if you genuinely connect with the 'patient'. But in general, there is very little attention and guidance given to people who have been made ill by a society which functions unhealthily. If you were to be more concerned about this social problem, you could save a huge amount of money in healthcare costs. You could then spend that money on prevention and coaching so these problems could be avoided. That would be a lot more humane.

Burn-out

If you radiate warmth and energy to your surroundings, you must make sure that your fire keeps burning, otherwise it will go out. To rekindle the flames, you have to take good care of yourself. That's the basis of good health and it allows your body to function well. That fire will keep burning if you stay true to yourself, and that keeps you in touch with your *Joy*. Obviously, you need to uphold your boundaries, and not ignore them. Be aware of what you can cope with; your energy supply is not inexhaustible. So make sure you set a good balance between giving and taking.

You might recognise yourself in one of the following situations:

> You feel as though other people don't accept who you really are.
> You're afraid that other people will reject or judge you.
> You're afraid of what others think of you.
> You do things which are unsuited to your competences, so you are constantly on your toes.

If you recognise yourself in one or more of these situations, there's a good chance you're going to do everything in your power to avoid them. You lose yourself in perfectionism because you believe that you will then be meeting the expectations of others. You're walking on eggshells. And because you're so concerned about others, you lose touch with yourself. You no longer know what you want, who you are, what your qualities or needs are or what life you want to lead.

You lose touch with your *Joy* and you're no longer living your own life, but that of someone else. It causes you to use up a lot of energy and you're running solely on willpower. You keep giving, but there's too little coming back. You get more and more tired and it' more and more of an effort to take action. The stress piles up. But you keep going. The energy needed to fuel your willpower is not coming from your *Joy* but from other parts of your body, resulting in you drifting further and further away from your feelings. In the end, you no longer recognise them. The door is locked, and you are unable to feel a warm connection with those close to you anymore. You shut yourself off from contact with others. If you do still have any energy left, you need it for yourself. You can no longer share it. This means that life gradually becomes less enjoyable and you don't look forward to going to work. This is often accompanied by the following symptoms: poorer concentration, loss of pleasure, worrying, insomnia, cynicism, mood swings, loss of the ability to empathise and avoidance of contact.

So a burn-out occurs if you pay too little attention to, and don't listen enough to your own emotional needs. You are constantly doing things which don't feel right and ignoring matters which are important to you. You forget what constitutes your pleasure, your talent, your relaxation, your food and your spare time. You keep on giving energy, but your fire is beginning to go out. You're ignoring your own boundaries and doing more than you can cope with over a long period. Just before the burn-out hits, you often have the feeling that your life is being lived for you. By your work, your responsibilities and by others. You've lost control over your own life. This makes you feel powerless and you try desperately to stay in control. At a certain point, shutting yourself off from others no longer helps. And suddenly it's over. You can't do anything anymore. Your energy source has dried up completely. You have a burn-out and you have landed in the Joyless situation.

The symptoms of burn-out are very similar to those of a depressive disorder, but they do differ. So it's very important to know what that difference is.

A burn-out is a disorder of your energy level. You want to tackle things, but you can't because you no longer have the strength to do so.

Depressive disorders manifest differently. You have no inclination to tackle things and nothing appeals to you. You are incapable of enjoying life.

So it's the difference between wanting to and being able to. That's why a depressive disorder requires a different approach to that of a burn-out. Because the symptoms are so similar, it's important to have a correct diagnosis. That will help you on your way.

Bore-out

A bore-out is a burn-out's little brother or sister. It occurs as a result of long-term boredom and work underload. You gradually become more and more exhausted and feel increasingly depressed. The fire inside is not burning well, it's not being stoked properly. The flame slowly goes out. A bore-out develops gradually; it's a real silent killer.

Maybe you have enough self-confidence but you're not being challenged to use your talent and personal strengths. You're working below your capacity. You have enough pleasure and energy but you're not being allowed, or don't need to tap into them for your work. And if you're not challenged, you start underperforming. No challenge, no satisfaction. Because you're bored, you start cutting corners and your *Joy* disappears.

You have enough self-confidence, so how could this happen? Is someone applying the brakes? You, or someone else? Ask yourself that. If it's someone else, your next step is to create a situation in which you will be able to use your talent and personal strengths and grow. You can open this up to discussion and indicate that you are ready for a next, new challenge. If you're not given that opportunity, it's best you start looking for a new job. And of course, you could always start up your own business.

Maybe you're the one applying the brakes. It's possible that your work activities are not enough in line with your personal sense of purpose. Maybe they were in the beginning, but now you've changed. Are you still doing what you love doing? Does your work contribute to that which you actually find important in the world? Can you still find that feeling in your work? Do you have the feeling that you're working on a mission? These are all questions you need to answer. If you answer them with 'No', it's hardly surprising you're feeling empty and useless.

Because if you can't express your *Joy*, you get frustrated and that makes you tired and down. The inner flames slowly die if they are starved of inspiration. You don't care, literally and figuratively, about the work you do; it no longer interests you and it shows. Why would it? After all, you're doing nothing with your talent or your wishes. It doesn't matter whether it's down to you, or someone else. You don't count. And if this period lasts a long time, you will land in the Joyless situation.

Recovering

As nasty as a burn-out is, and as long as the recovery takes, most people are glad afterwards that they experienced this complete breakdown. "I can only say that my burn-out undeniably did me good", writes Annegreet van Bergen in her book The Lessons of a Burn-out'. "I was able to change patterns that had crept in and teach myself a new way of living, with the result that I feel reborn." Once you have recovered, you're given a second chance. That's how it feels to almost everyone. And you change. "I now find myself a lot more important", one person says. "I no longer need to run with the pack, I've found my own strength", says another.

Many people only appreciate the feeling of *Joyfulness* when they're feeling really down. Life has made them face facts. They're ill, they feel unhappy, they no longer know exactly who they are, have no idea what they like, grind to a halt with a burn-out or feel depressed. All at once, they realise that they want to radically change their lives. I've heard the following statements so often: "This illness is the best thing that's ever happened to me.", or "It sounds crazy, but I wouldn't have missed it for the world." They're on a journey of discovery again and they've found the buried treasure: themselves. This is also my story. The need to change often occurs when you're feeling really low, when the suffering becomes great enough.

A burn-out is terrible but the fact is, it's only a symptom. And at the same time, it's a gift. It's a sign that you have followed a way of life and work which doesn't actually suit you and which has caused you to lose your pleasure and have no energy anymore. The burn-out is the consequence of the way of life.

Illness or a burn-out often puts an abrupt end to that pattern, but the change can also be gradual. One initial signal that people are becoming aware that they will have to change in order to be happy, is that they take a dislike to that forever 'having' to do things. They don't want to have to do things anymore. They don't want to have other people deciding what they have to do, and they want to break that pattern. The inner fire is not yet burning, but this is a spark. It's a sign that there's a feeling, deep inside, which is trying to fight its way out. So there's a ray of hope.

The way to *Joy* will be different for each individual, but everyone will need to get to know themselves before they can be themselves. You need to learn to feel again. To do that, everyone goes through their own process. You can aid this development through exercises, coaching and if necessary, therapy. And you can reinforce your own personal *Joy* by having fun with others.

If you are in the *Joyless* situation, it's important that you lay a new basis, the *Fertile soil*. It's wise to lay a foundation because you will have lost a lot of energy in the *Joyless* situation. Make sure you're physically in good condition, eat well and enjoy nature. These are the basic elements of every recovery and it's on this steady foundation that you will get to work. Because your mind has been overloaded with commotion, stimuli and information flows, you have lost touch with your body and feelings to a large extent. That's what you're going to restore, and there are several techniques which you can use. Mindfulness, as mentioned earlier, is one. Meditation and yoga can also help but with all these techniques, it's important that you learn to clear your mind so you can experience your uniqueness in the here and now. Let go of thoughts, stop fretting and don't worry about tomorrow. Trust that you are doing the right thing as long as you are doing it mindfully. This is also sometimes called 'grounding'.

Survival is naturally always a basic need, so it's vital that you give that some attention. Your body and your health, what you eat, feeling safe and sheltered and a degree of self-confidence form the basis of life. If these preconditions are missing, life is a desert. Not much grows on such ground. You need fertile soil to light your own fire.

That's why it's so awful if you lose touch with your own body and no longer feel safe. The only thing left to do is try to survive. Some people react by fighting, some by fleeing and others freeze. But the consequence for everyone is that you become anxious and the stress piles up. This might be due to personal circumstances or your working conditions or a combination of the two. One thing is certain, if you are anxious and stressed, you can't have fun and enjoy life.

You could use a helping hand during such a difficult time. A personal coach can guide you through the storm. I should point out that burn-out coaching requires a slightly different approach to that of a 'normal' coaching process. People with burn-out are overwhelmed by stress hormones and it's like a pinball machine in their heads, which means they need to be given more direction by the coach.

As a therapist, I have often been privileged to see my treatment contribute to the recovery. Those are wonderful experiences. Take for example the woman who came to see me six months after a burn-out. She immediately started to cry during the first session. During the intake interview, she had confided in me that she felt cold inside, and that she hadn't shed a single tear in the last six months. She couldn't get in touch with her emotions. Now she went straight to her feelings and the tears flowed. That's the power of physical work.

Naturally, the coachee also has to work on things. They have to demand their life back. They have to learn to again be aware of their living and working habits, to recognise signals given off by the body, to eat well and healthily and take enough exercise and relaxation.

Only then does the *Spark of Joy* have a feeding ground. If you have that basis and have found peace, you can start to look around you again. Maybe there's a spark and you get inspired by an idea, a book, a television programme or an encounter. That can be a signpost. The fact is, you can only be moved by something you love or find important. It could be the beginning of a new passion or mission.

Building up Joy

There are two main paths you can follow to stoke your *Spark of Joy* so that a *Flame of Joy*, or maybe even a small fire *(Blaze of Joy)* keeps burning. It comes down to breaking down old patterns and at the same time, replacing them with new behaviour.

Clearing limiting beliefs

Clearing limiting beliefs can be quite a lengthy process. You can see from my story about the last year that I was confronted several times with old beliefs and patterns which got in the way of my growth. For some people, there may be many such beliefs and patterns. You'll feel your *Joy* again for the first time when you distance yourself from beliefs imposed by and acquired from others. You will suddenly experience a deep realisation that you are living according to someone else's way of thinking instead of according to your own needs which you lost during childhood or the period after.

Once you realise this, you need to be 'reset', just like a computer which no longer functions properly. You may have to return to the factory setting you had when you were born. But perhaps the personal updates in your early childhood were less damaging and you can enter at a later age. The fact remains that many people have had software updates installed which don't support their own life programmes. There may also be viruses lurking in the system. They naturally have to be removed.

This recovery process is different for every individual because no two people are alike. The one similarity is that there are always limiting beliefs present, which you have taken on board during your life. Every child adapts to the norms, values and religious and other beliefs of the cultural group of which it is a part. You learn at a very early age that you must behave yourself, that's to say display behaviour according to norms which others impose upon you. This pressure is particularly great in your family. Children sense things and adapt unconsciously because they're vulnerable and dependent on the parents. They're afraid that if they don't adapt, their mother and father won't love them anymore. Once out of childhood, you adopt those imposed norms. Layer by layer, you construct an unauthentic ego, distancing yourself from your true self from an early age. The feeling of freedom you had as a child melts away like snow in the sun. Children's natural and playful behaviour is buried under a thick layer of learned and normative behaviour. My school playground story is a good example of that.

There are a number of beliefs which you take with you from your youth and which impair your self-confidence to a great degree. According to Annita Rogier (*Handboek coachen bij stress en burn-out*), the most commonly occurring are:

<u>Do your best.</u>

This causes insecurity. What is good enough and what must you achieve?

<u>Do me a favour.</u>

You learn to please others. So are you yourself worth enough?

<u>Be strong.</u>

You learn to toughen up. You don't let others see that you're tense or worried.

<u>Hurry up.</u>

This causes you to rush and make mistakes. You're also unable to enjoy what you have achieved.

<u>Be perfect.</u>

You never do things well enough. In the end, this will cause you to avoid tasks or challenges.

There are three ways that limiting beliefs can play a role in your way of thinking. First, the demands you make of yourself. We mentioned earlier having the feeling you must perform because otherwise you don't measure up as a person. This leads to shame, guilt feelings and depression. Second, the demands that other people have to meet. They must live up to your expectations and if they don't, you get angry. Last, you may be making demands of external circumstances. You feel things are not going the way you think they should. You become frustrated which in turn leads to you being less inclined to tackle matters yourself. But you don't do anything to change the situation.

Beliefs like these can be very persistent. They are ingrained, because you've gradually adopted them since you were a child. That's why you're often unaware of just how much they're restricting you.

A therapy such as the RET method (Rational Emotive Therapy) can help you to cope with stress and impediments. This therapy is used to ascertain how you deal with situations which make you tense and what your feelings and thoughts are then. Those thoughts are determined by the values, norms and opinions you were taught. They influence how you interpret a situation and how you react to that, emotionally and behaviourally. So if you can look at a situation from a different angle, the way you feel and react changes too. That can be a huge relief. It means you don't have to get stuck feeling anxiety, shame or guilt. Try a bit of self-examination and see if you can find out which thoughts and opinions play a dominant role in your life. Also check the extent to which they are restricting you. If necessary, you can replace those thoughts and opinions with others. Doing so could change your perception of certain events in a positive sense allowing you to behave differently. It's not the event which determines your life, but the way you view it!

So you can't change the event or situation, but you can learn to view it differently. To do that, you have to be aware of the thoughts which occur automatically in you. You can try to ascertain the content, how often it restricts you and whether you can change it.

However, if you really want to work on a thorough reset of your beliefs, conscious or otherwise, it's best to engage a good coach or therapist. They always have multiple methods they can use to mobilise the process of insight in you.

Building up Joy

Once you have recognised and changed your limiting beliefs, you will arrive in your authentic 'Being'. When you are able to experience your own core, your deepest being, you will rediscover your *Joy.* This is not a temporary escape from restless thinking, but a return to the person you always were but had lost sight of, because you swapped yourself and your 'Being' at an early age for the needs and expectations of others. *Joyfulness* reawakens the child in you. It concurs with what many forms of therapy call the Inner Child. When you have rediscovered that inner child, you will regain your energy because you're having fun. You'll feel playful and a smile will reappear on your face. Self-confidence and personal strength will return, and you will dare to set off on a journey of discovery, as a child does.

You can also stoke the flame of your inner *Joy* by playing, laughing, dancing or singing, together with others, because that makes it more fun. And as we will see later, healthier too. It lets you do what children regularly do: play together, sometimes in a circle. That's all it is. These activities allow the waves of *Joy* to break against the dikes you have built up to keep in your feelings, whether consciously or not. Those walls have made you a serious and responsible person who appears to have everything under control. But because of that, you have no fun anymore. Playing, laughing, dancing and singing in the here and now gives you energy once more. It starts to flow.

That fun could form the basis for you to rediscover and embrace your *Joy*. Once you have again felt how good it feels to play and have fun with others, you'll want to hold on to that feeling. You'll want to do things which are fun so that the energy will flow through your whole body again. That's also possible if you undertake an activity alone; as long as it fits with your inner 'Being'. If you dare to partly follow your feelings again and be yourself more often, you are in the phase of Blaze of Joy. You have energy and are enjoying yourself, but you're still keeping that to yourself. You're still feeling a little insecure. Sometimes it's easier than others, depending to a certain extent on the circumstances. Now you're just starting to feel some *Joy* inside, you're being a bit careful with it.

Zest for life is a godsend. It stems from the authentic 'Being' and is both the source and the consequence of *Joy*. If you're in the Blaze of Joy phase, zest for life is still fragile. There are often repressed feelings and a feeling of guilt standing in your way. You need to clear away those obstacles as quickly as possible; they are making you feel inhibited and unfree. Feelings must be allowed to flow and the dikes you have built up around your feelings are stopping you from leading the life that suits you and from being yourself. That's why you're not experiencing the joy of living.

When you get closer to your authentic self, a glimmer of zest for life occurs. Now you are able to take the next steps.

Taking into account your passion and mission, you deepen your connection to others and increase your creative capacity. It's actually that simple. You can follow the path to the recovery of *Joy* by giving what you have in you, even if you still have only a little energy. Do things for others which make them happy. The gratitude you receive will give you renewed energy. That feeling of *Joy* will come of its own accord if you give, act and work from your heart.

It's fantastic if you have rediscovered your *Joy* and you share it with those around you.
Our society desperately needs this.

Performing under pressure

You can feel the *Joy* in Picasso's painting 'The Youth Circle'; the happy, playful energy of youth splashing off the canvas. Happy, dancing young people, hand in hand, arms reaching for the sky. They are celebrating life together!"

Visual quote: Pablo Picasso; La Ronde de la Jeunesse (The Youth Circle), 1961.

The *Joyfulness* logo slightly resembles the Picasso painting. The arms are reaching towards the sky and those in the circle all have a different colour. No two people are the same. Thank goodness! You might even use a lot of imagination and see the logo as an extremely Cubist Picasso.

But the most important similarity is that both images show that there is nothing more wonderful than playing, laughing, dancing or singing in a group and joining together to make something which makes everyone happy. Doing fun things together is not only infectious, it creates mutual connection. As you celebrate life together, you build up positive energy. And when you're alone again, you continue to benefit from that; togetherness enriches you as an individual too. Do you remember what we said? *Joy* is the feeling that occurs inside you as a result of a positive exchange between you and the other person. It's giving *Joy* and receiving *Joy* at the same time.

Whatever happened to that playful childlike feeling of pleasure now we are adult? When do we ever stand in that happy circle of people these days? We all grow serious and pensive when we become adult. We lose our *Joy*. Why is it that as adults, we hardly ever play and laugh anymore, even though we did that so often as children?

Naturally, everyone experiences emotionally difficult times in their lives. No-one is spared that. And I'm tempted to say 'luckily'. Those intense times wakened me up. However, we often make difficult situations unnecessarily intense because of the behaviour we have been taught. That doesn't make the situation any better. You remain emotionally involved and before you know it, you feel like a victim. Once you take on that role, it's very hard to escape from it, even though it's not helping you at all. My experience, and fortunately that of others too, is that those deep lows can end up raising you to great heights if you just let go of control.

This is by no means a call to behave cheerfully while you're feeling worthless. Neither is it an attempt at ridding the world of all misery. Please just undergo your feeling as it comes. But be aware at the same time that you choose how to deal with that misery afterwards. Will you wallow in it or will you get on with your life? Those deeply emotional experiences can be a turning point. You can put that to good use by rediscovering your *Joy*, deep inside you, and feeling genuinely happy. That happiness will be coming from 'Being' and not from 'Appearing to be'.

Remember how much fun playing with other children was when you were a child? Whatever happened to that cheerful feeling in your childhood when you did fun things together? We do far too few things together. In the present society, it's all me, me, me! We scarcely work with other people anymore, and often see them as competition. Competition has become more important than collaboration. It has become a rat race for who is the best, the smartest, the wealthiest or the most beautiful.

That's the message we are given from the beginning of our lives. You have to be better than the others and everything is an individual competition. You can forget the idea of achieving something together. You can join a club, of course, but there too, particularly in the case of a sports club, competition between people is central. Logical, as such, but in the worst cases, it's all about winning or losing; who's the best. That applies not only to the team, but also to your share in that team. We're only happy if we have won. And heaven forbid one team member should screw up in the competition. They'll be in big trouble! It's no fun running after a ball in these conditions, even though these activities are meant to encourage relaxation and teamwork.

Naturally, there's nothing wrong with giving a great performance, whether individually or in a team. That's given us some wonderful things. But competitiveness has become important even in everyday situations. It's totally unnecessary and it puts us under constant pressure. And it's perfectly possible to give a great performance while you're relaxed and having fun. Especially if you do it together and combine all the diverse talents.

But there is an unnecessarily competitive form of performance which exercises a very negative pressure to perform and that's not the same as a healthy performance. When you perform well, you achieve something, but when you're pressured to perform, you don't do yourself or others justice.

Unfortunately, there is a lot of pressure to perform these days. At work, at home and even when playing sports or taking part in hobbies. We have to keep an awful lot of balls in the air and it's becoming increasingly difficult to do so. More than anything, we like to share all our activities with the whole world, through social media. That allows us to demonstrate that we have an absolutely fantastic life; we're adventurous, we dine out a lot and we're oh so happy. We have an awful lot of appearances to keep up, and if that means you constantly have to be on your toes, at some point that will come back and bite you. If problems occur, or if we have demanded too much of ourselves, our whole world falls apart. Stress builds and you're ashamed because you're unable to meet all the requirements and expectations, while others seemingly are. That means you have failed.

Afterwards, you're worried sick trying to work out what's causing it and how you can get back on your feet. But if you're under a lot of stress, you can't think straight.

And if you're still actually feeling anything at all, it's probably guilt and shame. It really bothers you that you're leaving your colleagues at work in the lurch, because you're overstrained.

Performing under pressure

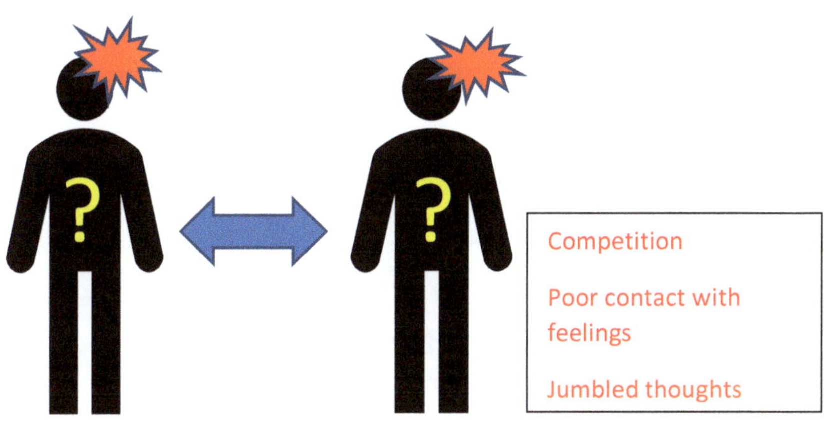

And yet almost all of us started out as children who had fun playing. We were able to explore the world around us and experience things freely, and through play. That's how you learned as a child what you liked and what you were good at. When children play, they don't think or worry about what might happen later that day or what happened yesterday. They just have fun, in the moment. Their focus is on discovering, laughing, having fun and playing. They look for excitement and often not on their own, but with each other. They experience a life that is completely in the here and now. They marvel at everything they see.

Children love to play together and don't need Mindfulness to help them with the here-and-now experience. I can imagine that for adults, on the other hand, Mindfulness is a good way of unwinding. Especially nowadays. The fact is that people now are always overly busy, and they don't play anymore. It shocks me when I see Mindfulness courses being organised for children. And it's not just the odd one: if I search 'Mindfulness for children' in Google, I get no less than 2.5 million hits. How many children do we have here in the Netherlands? Are they no longer able to just be children?

> *"The nice thing is that children are actually generally very mindful. Often, they live so much in the moment that they can get completely involved in the cat rubbing up against their legs as they're on their way to bed. Or in a piece of paper, a drop of water, in anything actually. They forget where they were going because at that moment, something more important grabs their attention. Nice! But sometimes less than convenient for their parents.*
>
> *Sadly, many children lose this 'mindful' attitude as they grow up. Just like you, they have a busy schedule and are no longer aware of the here and now. You can help them to unwind."*
>
> **Ouders van Nu (Today's Parents magazine)**

How is this possible? As parents, we're going to help our children unwind with a course in Mindfulness, even though children are mindful by nature. Isn't it absurd that 370 schools in the United Kingdom have added Mindfulness lessons to their curricula?

That's just unbelievable! Today's parents and today's children are all under pressure and stressed out. They're not living in the here and now. Naturally, the idea of giving children extra support in this hectic society is to be praised. I can definitely see benefits to be gained from Mindfulness and it helps too, without a doubt. But let's be honest: we won't be changing anything about our modern society, which has got completely out of hand. Mindfulness is purely palliative in this case. We're making our children ill through our stressed and competitive way of living, only to subsequently give them a serving of Mindfulness. Put bluntly: it's as though you beat your child and then 'help' them by giving them an aspirin for their headache.

Why don't we just let children be children? Why do we need relaxation techniques to help them unwind? Why can't we just let them have fun together and relax and get into the here and now that way. That's the natural way. Playing is mentally and physically healthy and relaxing. And it's done together!

And the time in which children can be children is already so short. They go to school to learn and are gradually taught that thinking and being competitive are the most important skills you can have in life. Naturally, thinking is important, but these days it takes up such a prominent place that we are in danger of losing our intuition and our ability to play and discover and they can be so valuable.

By unnecessarily focusing too much on the competition and a school's scores, the value of individual differences between children gets lost. Every child is unique and deserves to be valued for that. You're not less valuable just because you're less proficient in a particular subject than other children are. It just means that your talent lies elsewhere. It is however important that the talent can also be seen and valued. That's quite difficult, since the Dutch school system has set standards which every child has to meet. They get tested on that. But maybe your talent lies somewhere else completely and can't be tested, or just isn't tested.

In addition to the influence of school, children are taught norms and values at home which establish themselves as beliefs in their way of thinking. The parents too have been raised with performing under pressure and competition. So performing under pressure is being emphasised from all sides. "Do your best!" "Stop playing around!" "Learning and working are not playing!"

I recently spoke with a young mother in my practice, whose daughter goes to primary school. This mother had been to a standard ten-minute interview with the teacher to see how things were going for the child at school. To the mother's surprise, the teacher started

Research shows that many teenagers and young adults feel under pressure to perform. This trend only seems to be growing. In 2018, three thousand students took part in a study by Windesheim University of Applied Sciences. Of those questioned, 68.9% said they often, or very often, had problems with pressure to perform. This number was only 62% in 2016. University psychologists are more frequently treating students who have serious and complex problems. For that reason, they are referring more and more young people to the family doctor or even to the local mental health authority.

The prevalent pressure to perform causes children and young adults to become increasingly alienated from a natural 'Being'. This over-emphasis on learning and competition means that the pleasure we take in doing things gradually diminishes. We are taught to do our best and not taught to be ourselves or enjoy life. Our intuitive capacity declines and our creative powers are extinguished. Everything has to be done perfectly. But that way, we will never reach our *Joy,* never mind feel happy in ourselves.

The societal burn-out

The motives behind our performance-oriented western society are mainly economic in nature. That gradually took over as the religious experience and church organisations began to disappear from the community. The amount of economic growth achieved has become increasingly determining for the degree of success of our society.

That's logical to a certain extent, since everyone wants to have some level of welfare and it has given us a great deal in the last decade. Most inhabitants of the western world have basic safety, basic good health and basic accommodation. And everyone is given an education. So inhabitants are provided with most of their basic needs. That's something to be proud of and grateful for.

But on the other hand, it demands an awful lot of every one of us. From the very beginning of our lives, we are groomed to capture our place in this society. At school, during further education and at work, it is imprinted on us what we have to do, and sometimes who we have to be, in order to be successful and take part in this economic rat race. More than anything, we learn to deliver achievements and compete with others. They are individual achievements for which you are given a grade in your school report. These grades are supposed to demonstrate that you have the necessary basic knowledge. During further education, you acquire extra specialist knowledge. You need all that knowledge in order to be able to contribute to society.

So the child at play soon disappears into the background. In the education system, you get grades for your achievements and they are better if you work hard at your studies. You must use your brain. Learning through play, experimenting and discovering are disregarded. Performance takes precedence over pleasure and passion and you have to adhere to that, otherwise you'll be left behind.

This strong performance approach and the specialised professional and educational options from which you have to choose from quite a young age, cause your own personal strength, passion and talent to disappear more and more into the background. Which of us is strong enough to survive this field of influence? People who don't adapt to the social rules and family norms - parents always want the best for their children - have difficulty holding their own. They are often bullied, and it doesn't take long before the things at which they excel are no longer acknowledged.

Those who start jobs after finishing their studies, must perform yet again. You take a job because after the study, you want to earn some money and stand on your own two feet. It's not something granted to everyone, but you'd really like to have a job that suits you and do something you enjoy doing. That's if you at least have an idea. It's been shown that this is not at all self-evident. Everybody knows what they want, but there are no vacancies. So they settle for another job for the time being. The danger is that because of the money you are earning, or because it's convenient, you stay in that job. You no longer look for the job that would suit you so well. And with that, you lose your *Joy*.

Once you do have work, you are again confronted with pressure to perform. You wonder what is expected of you and whether you are doing your work well enough. That will be defined by your production, your knowledge and the competences you need for it. If a performance review reveals that you score less than a passing grade on a competence, you will be given a certain amount of time to improve on this. If you don't manage that, you may well be looking for another job. You are typically forced to adapt your behaviour to well-established standards of competence. You must do your best to improve them, even though that's not where your personal strength or passion lie. There's still too little focus on how the company can best use your personal strength and passion; if necessary, by giving you other work to do. Luckily, a shift has been seen recently, with talent management on the rise. However, many companies and organisations still don't know how to approach this or are stuck in the old way of thinking.

If you're different, you attract attention and may be out of place. People are often bullied just because they are different to others. Sadly, there seem to be a great many instances of bullying behaviour. We've known for a long time that it happens at schools, but the fact that it also happens in the workplace originally came as a surprise. In fact, no fewer than one in ten employees suffers badly from bullying. People are ignored and excluded, made fun of and even intimidated. There's also a lot of gossiping. It's just shocking to think that roughly half of bullied employees have serious stress-related or burn-out problems as a result of this bullying behaviour. I see this bullying behaviour as a symptom of the fact that we now find competition and pressure to perform so important. It's a well-known fact that bullies bully because they want to feel superior to others. They have problems at home, at school or at work and are often unable to keep up, or meet the demands being made of them. They feel vulnerable, and they don't want to feel that way at all. They compensate by behaving dominantly towards those who are weaker. And anyone who doesn't fit in the group because they have unique characteristics in terms of appearance or personality, becomes the victim.

The consequence of this work culture is that many people are unhappy in what they are doing: "I have to go to work again". Many people are caught up in a web of work, earning money to pay the mortgage and other bills and looking after the children.

Some of them have a voice, deep inside, calling out for a different way of life. They'd like to do something else but don't know how to go about it. Emotionally, they are stuck in their responsibilities and they hang on in there until the pressure just becomes too much. Then suddenly, changes have to be made! A few even emigrate. Television programmes such as 'Wanted Down Under' which broadcast these adventures are watched by many viewers. Apparently, it strikes a chord with a lot of people.

There is also a group of people who feel empty; they are dissatisfied with their lives but have no idea what it is they would like. They haven't found their passion, which is logical, since they have never paid it any attention. I see young people in my practice who are not yet thirty and already have burn-out symptoms. They're exhausted and no longer have any idea of what to do with their lives. They wonder how they can get back their pleasure and neither know nor understand themselves anymore. They have been stuffed full of their parents' beliefs and the knowledge they acquired at school but there has been no attention paid to the most important knowledge: self-knowledge.

There are others who avoid their feelings and give everything they have for the performance, the compliments it gets them and the feeling of pride that gives. That approval makes them go even further and they become increasingly addicted to their work. They have no time to unwind and lose sight of the important things in life. When they go on holiday, they're often ill for the first few days.

In this era of information, people can no longer cope with the constant stream of information being fired at them. We are bombarded with all kinds of data which we have to process and place. Our minds are working overtime. We analyse, think about it overnight, look for solutions and if we cannot solve it on our own, we hold a brainstorming session with a group. There's a storm in our heads and we can't get it to subside. In many cases, people have become heads with bodies which are no more than appendages. They're always thinking or worrying, being stimulated continuously and from all sides, constantly suffering unhealthy stress and they've lost all contact with their bodies and their feelings. And another important point: in this digital world, in which communication takes place to a large extent through social media, the attention and compassion between people has been side-tracked.

I also spent a long time right in the middle of such a situation. I had also become a head with a body which was no more than an appendage. Every day, so much information was fired at me that I simply no longer knew where to store it and how to process it. I'm actually a people person by nature, but that was no longer obvious to other people. I was regularly being told that I had become hardened. Often, by the time I got home, my brain's hard disk was completely full, and I had no room to store anything else. That meant I was no longer capable of good contact with others, even though that's something very important to me. However, you get used to it after a while, and that's the really strange thing. I mean, I knew that what I was doing wasn't right, but I kept on doing it anyway. What choice did I have? How could I have done things differently? Naturally, it didn't feel right, so I was constantly searching for other stimuli. I was continually working on change and renewal, because that meant I wasn't feeling that I was in fact stuck. Since I still had activities outside work which helped redress the balance and provided energy, I was able to keep up this way of life for a long time. It felt as though I had a split personality, but I kept going anyway. I'm pretty sure I did not radiate *Joy* in any way. Not that I was aware of that.

When I suddenly found myself in a different situation, I did radiate *Joy*. A few years ago, a great many refugees came to Europe, fleeing the war in Syria. The influx to the Netherlands was so great that a lot of emergency shelter had to be organised. I was made responsible for that in one of the municipalities. It was a huge challenge. I had to find answers to all sorts of questions. What is needed in terms of location, food and medical facilities?

How many professionals and volunteers do we need? How should we organise this together?

I will never forget the arrival of the first group in a bus filled with misery, and my gaze went immediately to a father, mother and their two toddlers. None of them had coats and they wore flip-flops. And it was November! Everything they owned was in a single plastic carrier bag. And these were the people some were calling fortune seekers?! I had to give a speech, welcoming them, and telling them about the procedure and the house rules, with the help of an interpreter. While she was interpreting, I had a chance to observe the group. I will never forget the exhausted looks on their faces. Who is this man? What does he want from us? Where are we? What will happen to us here? How long will we stay here? The looks which went from hope to fear and back to hope.

Luckily, everything went well with their reception. I personally felt completely at home with my task and responsibility. This was work with a mission: meaningful work because you could immediately see what it provided for the people who needed it. And it was working with passion: this challenge suited me perfectly. I enjoyed it and I was good at it. There was a wonderful work atmosphere among the colleagues who did their share and the staff of other organisations. No-one complained or grumbled. Everyone just got on with it and we all worked really hard. I was at the shelter location for ten days in a row, from the early morning till midnight. I didn't mind. It revived me. When I popped by my usual workplace in between times, my colleagues were amazed. They were seeing a completely different Johan; energetic and radiant. Clearly, that work gave me *Joy*. It was written on my face and visible in my whole attitude.

Going back to my old ways was difficult after this experience. I now knew what I was missing. My need to genuinely work together with other people and to give employees the chance to use their talent, became increasingly important to me. I had come up with a mission for myself and the organisation and wanted to change both. But to do that, everyone had to be on the same page, and that was too much to ask. Competition turned out to be stronger than collaboration. But I couldn't settle into my old pattern anymore. I started making impossible demands of myself and completely ignoring my boundaries. My body rebelled and I was back again, close to a burn-out.

That was the situation when I started on my story in this book. I'm sure I'm not the only person to land in such a situation. How many people have too many demands made of them? How many people are swamped with information they can no longer process? How many people are doing work which doesn't suit them? How many people dread going to work because they feel unsafe there? I think there are a great many. And with that, I believe we have a huge problem in our society.

In The Netherlands, 16% percent of workers are suffering from stress and burn-out symptoms. 40% of university staff indicates that they feel socially unsafe at work. All this is caused by poor leadership, bullying, gossiping, intimidation, abuse of power and fierce competitiveness.

In the UK, in 2018, 595,000 workers are suffering from work-related stress, depression or anxiety (new or long-standing). Stress, depression and anxiety caused by: workload - 44%, lack of managerial support - 14%, violence, threats and bullying - 13%.

(Source: www.hse.gov.uk/statistics/lfs/index.htm)).

Should we just think it normal that 19.7% of people in the UK aged 16 and over showed symptoms of anxiety or depression?

The society we created together is clearly suffering from a burn-out. It's general knowledge that we are exhausting nature with our system, but I would assert that we are also exhausting ourselves. The aforementioned rise in people with a burn-out is a symptom of a social system which is unhealthy, due to the bombardment of information, the competition, the pressure to perform and the over-regulation by way of all sorts of protocols and unnecessary registrations. The focus in work needs to be on people again. They should be central, with attention to focus, particularly in the care sector! We must put an end to competition and intimidation at work. It's time for *Together*. I wish every employer could experience the challenge of organising shelter for a group of refugees.

There is no equilibrium in our society. There is no longer a balance between work and rest, between enjoying and being obliged, between individual and together, intelligence and feelings, system and people, money and meaningfulness, between giving and taking. That has grave and visible consequences at both a societal and an individual level.

Sadly, this social monster keeps charging on and on because those who turn their backs on it are not organised. They are all individuals who go off in search of a new balance, reading one self-help book after another. But they're all solitary, which is why it's time we made a common noise, to show we want to do things differently. Together. New dogmas are the last thing I want, but I would like to see more balance in everything. More *Joy,* more *Together*, more feelings, compassion and attention, more creativity, more meaningfulness and more intuition.

Part 5   Brightening our world

If you are working on something exciting that you really care about you don't have to be pushed.

The vision pulls you.

Steve Jobs

From looking in to looking after

Of course it's logical that an unbalanced life full of stress cannot be maintained. If you are trapped in such a situation, you want to escape.

So now we're all looking for happiness and high points. Happiness becomes a goal in itself. Because happiness isn't just there for the taking, and because the philosophy of economics has so invaded our way of thinking, we think we can buy happiness. So we go off in search of wealth and beauty.

For the latter, we are prepared to do anything to make sure we look perfect in our selfies. We think we're _so_ important! Research by The American Academy of Facial Plastic and Reconstructive Surgery shows that half of all people undergoing procedures is under thirty years old. Young people buy injectables as easily as they buy new clothes.

One warm weekday, we were at the beach and watched in amazement as a young couple with two toddlers spent a lot of time making selfies in all sorts of tough or seductive poses. Meanwhile, the toddlers were walking into the sea without mother or father even noticing. We were there for two hours, and the parents didn't play with the children at all.

And as I was writing this experience down, I received an email. It was from a large online store: 'Tomorrow is National Glamour Day! Fill in your wish list now!'

Surely it must clear by now that appearance never makes you happy. Naturally, it's lovely if you look good, have nice things and can do pretty much anything you want to do. But the statistics are unforgiving. People in the United States have not become happier in the last fifty years, even though the standard of living has risen.

Apparently, the majority of people look for happiness outside themselves. They believe that fun events will make them happy, but that is generally short-lived. The emptiness returns and that's not a good feeling. So you go looking as soon as possible for something else to make you 'happy'. In the end, it becomes a vicious circle. You want more, and more often. You need increasingly more parties to give you a feeling of happiness, in the same way as an alcoholic needs increasingly more beer or wine to achieve the same effect, the intoxication. It has become an addiction.

This is the explanation for why there are so many thrill-seekers these days. They go to the limits, because they crave the adrenaline boost that they get from high points. That gives them a fantastic feeling. You see videos on social media, showing extreme daredevilry, sometimes also resulting in death. The leading players feel so magnificent that they think they are immortal.

This also explains television programmes such as 'Wanted Down Under' or 'Escape to the Chateau', which show couples or families starting up new lives in a sunny country. They don't know what to do in their current lives to make themselves happy and so they take action. These programmes give the viewer a good idea of the lengths to which people will go to change their lives. They often go back to a more basic lifestyle because they have learned that luxury did not bring them happiness. But just how many French chateaux can you turn into Bed and Breakfasts? How many tearooms can you have in Tuscany?

People who don't move away look for other forms of relaxation, the simplest of which of course is just to buy a statue of Buddha at the garden centre and give it a nice place in your garden. If nothing else, you make it clear that you're working on meaningfulness and wellness. It shows that, despite your busy life, you are well-balanced. That you live very consciously. Often against your better judgement.

Similarly, Mindfulness has become incredibly popular in recent years. Mindfulness means being open and aware in the here and now: you learn to observe what is happening in the here and now, without judgement or bias. It helps you calm the constant commotion in your mind by making you aware of your own physical experiences and thoughts, rather than responding immediately and automatically. Training sessions, meditation and other exercises in focus are the way to achieve this.

Mindfulness

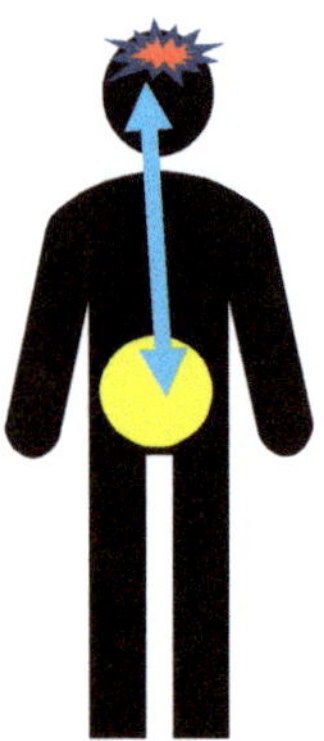

Employers and healthcare insurers are now also embracing Mindfulness in their search for answers to the huge problems caused by stress and burn-out, which are quite simply costing them an awful lot of money. And since money is the driving force in business operations, they are apparently even prepared to embrace less obvious solutions.

Mindfulness helps a great many people, but it's aimed at the individual and society is already so individualistic. There are however other ways of being in the here and now, methods which give you creative energy and a lot of pleasure. Specifically by carrying out the activities together with others, just as children do, running around and playing games together, in the here and now. Of course, that doesn't apply to the children already taking Mindfulness lessons.

I think a lot of people recognise that feeling of wanting to show others your personal strength because that pleasure comes from the inside. To be appreciated for who you are, deep inside, and not initially because you perform well under pressure which might make someone else happy, but not you. To get energy from being asked or challenged to join others working on a worthy goal. Because of your personal qualities. You can be your innermost self and people actually appreciate you too.

It's wonderful to use your personal strength to show who you are and, on that basis, make a contribution that makes a difference. You respond to your personal *Joy* and experience your own, profound, innermost feeling of happiness. You feel the fire inside that you want to radiate, simply because you can't not share it. And with that, you warm up and light the world. There's a smile on your face again and you feel it inside too. When you're feeling like this, you're less likely to have a burn-out or suffer symptoms of depression unless you really throw your energy around. There is a limit to its supply after all. You no longer need temporary kicks because you need them to compensate for the discontent inside. You no longer have to live from one weekend to the next, or from one holiday to the next.

Mindfulness and meditation can indeed help you to take the first and necessary step towards recovery, the step that takes you out of your mind, full of restless thoughts and worry about problems and their solutions. This is a very important, but difficult assignment for many people. That indicates the importance of meditation and Mindfulness and explains their success. It's a relief, managing to briefly escape the commotion, thanks to these techniques and this helps you lay a foundation. However, in my experience this is not enough to help you get the true feeling of happiness. Inner peace is wonderful, and I was always very glad when thinking or worrying was reduced to a minimum in my head. But later, I realised that inner happiness and enthusiasm are the things that really help you move forward. And they occur of their own accord when you are doing something that gives you pleasure. If you can be your true self, and reveal that to others, you can then connect with them. You let them share in your *Joy* and that is so contagious that it can lead to amazing partnerships. For me, that's the real feeling of *Joyfulness*.

You could describe *Joyfulness* as a logical consequence of Mindfulness. *Joyfulness* lets you experience the flow from a state of 'Being'. The characteristics are movement, pleasure and creativeness, so you don't have to just sit still or concentrate. With *Joyfulness*, you break through the individualism which plays such a major role in the current selfie culture. With *Joyfulness,* you experience the most pleasure by being and creating together. *Joyfulness* takes you to that playful feeling you had as a child. You rediscover your inner child. And that child likes to play with other children!

Current situation	Mindfulness	Joyfulness
Stress	Tranquillity	Pleasure
Competition	Individualism	Compassion
Pressure to perform	Present	Creativeness
Rational thinking	Focus	Intuition

You don't perform from *Joyfulness*, you create playfully and you do it in the here and now. You're not actually aiming for a feeling of happiness, it's a state of 'Being'. You don't have to meet any demands or expectations others might have. Neither do you have to compare yourself to others or be compared with them to achieve something which is actually of no use to you.

> *Achieving happiness is not an achievement*
>
> *So don't make a goal of achieving happiness*

Don't aim for happiness at all. It's not a goal. Being in pursuit of happiness will not make you happy. This is a strange idea in a society in which so many people are convinced that you will always succeed as long as you do your best. Or that you deserve happiness, simply because you do your best and work hard. Maybe we aim our arrows at happiness because it's the highest asset. In the end, you'll find that the arrows miss their target, however hard you try. That's frustrating!

If you're accustomed to delivering performances, the idea of automatically feeling happy just by being yourself is a bizarre one. In fact, that feeling of happiness is the result of you finding your authentic 'Being' and sharing that with others.

In an interview for brainwash.nl, the Belgian psychiatrist Dirk de Wachter gives a very good description of the currently predominant way of thinking such as 'achieving everything on your own' and 'happiness as a goal in itself'.

'Back to happiness. Is it just in recent years that we've become so obsessed with it?'

"I don't think you can indicate a particular turning point. This has been going on for some time. It has to do with the secularisation of the world. We no longer have a God with whom to fatefully link our unhappiness. We've all become responsible for our own 'me' lives. Our

society seems to have gone overboard in 'me-ness', in an overvalued notion of autonomy, in 'I can do everything on my own'. The rise of the individual, which is a good thing, began during the Age of Enlightenment. But it has since tipped over into an excess of achieving everything alone. We are expected to make our own success. And if that success doesn't come, we feel we have failed."

"And that's how happiness has become a goal in itself."

"Yes, absolutely. That's my assertion. And it's not a good thing. Don't get me wrong, I would grant everyone a happy life, but I believe that happiness can be a side-effect of a good life; a meaningful life, lived together with others, a caring life, a life that is shared. Look after yourself, look after your health and your surroundings, look after other people. That way, happiness will be there of its own accord, and in a much more fundamental way that party-time happiness would be. It's a feeling of fulfilment: this is right, this is how my life can be. When happiness becomes a goal, an obsessional goal, things can go wrong. Naturally, life can be difficult from time to time, but the effect is lessened. You can cope with it, because you know you are cherished."

"So, a bit more commitment then?"

"Yes, commitment to yourself and to others, but also in the form of engagement. Having the feeling that what you do is meaningful and that the world acknowledges it. Author Gerard Reve wrote that too at the end of De Avonden, as Frits van Egters is reflecting on his life: 'It has been seen, it has not gone unnoticed.' I believe that humans have a deep need to be meaningful. Not that everyone has to be famous or have a huge number of Facebook friends, but that you feel connected with those close to you, with family and friends. It's about caring and being cared for. If that can be achieved, we feel happy in that fundamental way."

Belgian psychiatrist Dirk de Wachter, 2018, www.brainwash.nl

I'll say it one more time, very briefly: 'Happiness will come if you move From Looking in to Looking After!'

> *Joy can be real only if people look upon their lives as a service and have a definite object in life outside themselves and their personal happiness.*
>
> Leo Tolstoy

Never stop playing

So as adults, we have submitted completely to performing under pressure and competition. Everything we do has to have a concrete goal, with a measurable result, we have to be personally really very good at it and it must be finished in next to no time. That's pressure. We've got carried away by result-orientation and perfectionism. And it's sapping our strength. There's almost nothing we still do just because it's fun and feels good, even though the latter is precisely what would lead to success. Obviously, it's to be expected that we get more responsibility when we become adult. In addition to work, we have to run a household and raise children who also have to be taken to swimming lessons, birthday parties, judo, gymnastics and guitar lessons. We are drowning in 'having to' and forget how to just play and have fun.

And often, if we do something for ourselves, we want to see results immediately. It seems as though we seldom do something just for fun. When are you still able to just hang out?

Speaking of results: the term SMART is now embedded in most companies. It's a method used to book results and achieve goals. The letters stand for Specific, Measurable, Achievable (or Assignable), Realistic (or Relevant) and Time-bound.

WIKIPEDIA: 'The SMART principle is management or educator jargon for setting up and checking goals simply and unambiguously. Technicians and engineers at companies such as Philips started using the term in the 1990s to get their managers to give clear assignments.'

When you read this, you know immediately that this is a one-sided, rational method. It suits the way of thinking of technicians and engineers. The approach is probably extremely useful in that world so I don't want to judge it, but it's now being applied all the time, in all sorts of work situations, even those which should revolve around people. So it's high time there was a revaluation of the creative and innovative power of playing and improvising. That won't be easy, since SMART is perfectly in line with the culture of performing under pressure. But neither SMART nor performing under pressure suit the changed needs of these times anymore. We desperately need a different approach. Give people scope and confidence and work will once again become fun and meaningful! A shift from SMART to PLAY will motivate employees and give them the chance to work from the heart rather than having to fill in forms.

A study (Perry et al) carried out in 2000 showed that Playfulness has a direct effect on the development of: Creativity and self-expression; Teamwork; Communication/ negotiation/compromise; Decision-making and problem solving; Inventing/developing skills; Development of intrinsic interests; Self-reliance and self-confidence; Regulation of emotion and empathy; Social interaction.

Looking at this list, you might wonder if there's anything at all on which play does not have a positive effect. Playing clearly contributes positively to basic personal skills and improves the work culture. Playing is therefore an essential element in our lives.

Tine Schellekens, psycho-dynamic paediatric psychotherapist and doctoral researcher at the Catholic University in Liège, describes playing more in terms of a mindset than a concrete activity: a way of thinking which involves carrying out activities based on pleasure and experiencing no pressure. And the great thing is that this mindset leads to success in the end.

> *Play covers everything which you enjoy doing and in which you experience no pressure whatsoever.*

Clearly, this mindset of playing leads to success, increases creativity, ensures good social relationships and is extremely healthy. So why do we play so little as adults, either at work or in our private lives? Working without pressure and based on play: it's actually very simple. Do we realise what we're missing together? Why did we let it get this far? Are we afraid that we won't get any work done, because people are just generally lazy? In organisations and businesses, staff have to register how long they spend on particular activities. Stop that! Enthusiastic, passionate people who work because they enjoy it always do more than people you monitor and keep trapped in administrative hassle.

> *We don't stop playing because we grow old*
> *we grow old because we stop playing*
>
> George Bernard Shaw

And please stop believing that you must achieve a result when you do something. Your goal is not to get something, or to want to be the best. That won't give you strength. The goal should be dynamic. You want to achieve something from a source you feel deep inside, but without knowing exactly what the result will look like. If you can do that, you will take pleasure in what you're doing and feel connected, both to other people and to the whole. You will experience no time pressure, since you no longer have to achieve something within a certain time period. You will discover that developments happen of their own accord; you act based on the feeling of *Joy*. You will notice that in such moments, you've actually progressed much further than you could ever have dreamed. This has happened to me so often recently. You once again become the intrepid explorer you used to be as a child, and you enjoy the unexpected discoveries you make and the adventures you have. It's exciting and fun. 'The vision pulls you.'

During a hiking tour in the mountains of Nepal, I walked a beautiful route. The guidebooks described how you could walk from one main village to the next. Almost all the hikers competed to see who could make the fastest time, instead of taking the opportunity to enjoy the nature, the people and the tiny mountain villages. If you met a hiker, their only conversation was about how far they had travelled and how long it had taken them. They were missing so much. My most wonderful experience was spending the night in a house where no tourists came, because they were all lodging in the main villages. I slept in a small room together with people in their home. They invited me to eat with them and we ate a simple meal while their children sat on the floor doing their homework by the light of an oil lamp. It was an unforgettable scene and I can still see it before me. All the rushed, competitive hikers were spending the night in one large hostel, eating pizzas or hamburgers. Did they enjoy the authentic Nepal?

The power of Together

'What do you mean, abandon competitiveness and tackle things together? It's about the survival of the fittest, isn't it?' This is the kind of answer you will probably hear if you comment critically on our competitive society. When Charles Darwin wrote about the survival of the fittest, he was not referring to 'the might is right'. The meaning has been taken completely out of context and in the past, even used to justify social wrongdoing.

> 'However, an organism need not necessarily be the 'fittest' in order to have a better chance of survival than others. Better flight behaviour, better camouflage or higher intelligence can sometimes increase the chances of survival and ensure that an organism is 'the fittest'. In general, an organism with characteristics which make interaction with the challenges of the surroundings more efficient and more effective, will have a better chance of survival.
>
> **Wikipedia: survival of the fittest**.

In his subsequent book, *The Descent of Man*, written in 1871, British nature researcher, biologist and geologist Darwin emphasised the altruistic instincts in animals and humans. According to him, these instincts are more developed in humans than in animals, so that we are inclined to protect others. Darwin says that even if this behaviour were to lead to some weakening of the race, we should just accept that. The need that people feel to work together and take each other into consideration is precisely what has ensured that humans have evolved further than other species.

Long ago, these instincts formed the basis for a species to survive. This altruistic instinct is even a part of the human primitive brain.

Have we forgotten the power of *Together*? Are we no longer aware of the importance of mutual contact and collaborative partnerships? It seems to me that a dissenting opinion against the increasingly strong selfie culture which worships the 'Me', is desperately needed. More and more often, we hide behind our smartphones, even in the company of other people. Even more ridiculous: being in touch with each other through social media and apps while we are actually all in the same space. It has been proven, more than once, that we have less and less eye contact with each other in recent years. That's a pity, since you need to look at each other roughly sixty to seventy percent of the time to make an emotional connection. Five years ago the figures were between thirty and sixty percent, and they have presumably fallen further since then. It's a shame, because eye contact is incredibly important since it reinforces the mutual connection and gives a feeling of trust. Those are crucial elements for a good collaboration. Eye contact also makes people act and behave more socially and altruistically.

> *Bringing all your people together, both as individuals and collaborators, increases empathy and mutuality. Even if it's just for half an hour at the beginning of a workshop, collaboration is important to help overcome barriers of shyness and reticence for some participants.*
>
> *At the same time, play can take the edges off some of the tensions that emerge in our social hierarchies.*
>
> **The CEOmagazine.com 24 februari 2016**

There's a good reason why the power of *Together* is such an important component of *Joyfulness*. Clearly, you experience *Joy*, taking pleasure from being in the here and now, most intensely when together with other people. Having fun and working on something together provides a strong feeling of unity, as does frequent eye contact. Doing things together allows you to build up energy and inspire and motivate each other. Together is always stronger than alone. Together, you build towards a common group experience, sharing activities such as playing, cooking, laughing, dancing, singing, playing percussion and making music. You can see it happening even if you are not visually oriented. Personally, I immediately see a scene in which the villagers of an indigenous tribe are dancing in a circle around the fire. In that community, the many celebrations and rituals ensure mutual connection, trust and safety. That's a form of self-preservation for these isolated tribes.

Western society no longer has rituals like this anymore. You may see a hint of them at a village gathering, but such rituals have disappeared to a large extent from our society, certainly in the cities. And with that disappearance, we have also forgotten the positive power which results from those rituals. These activities are in stark contrast to our individualistic daily activities, because those rituals are played and carried out together. It's not about an achievement. There's no element of competition involved so it's safe for all participants. It doesn't matter whether you laugh loudly or quietly, whether your vocal technique is good or not. All these communal activities are related. For example, singing and laughing are very close to each other. They're not separate activities; they flow into each other.

It's only recently that scientific research in the West has confirmed that such group activities are really beneficial to people. These activities appear to be extremely healthy in more ways than one, at an individual level and at a group level, they ensure positive group forming and strong ties.

The great thing about all this is that if you take part in these activities, they contribute to the personal development and health of all individual participants. A huge amount of energy is released in doing activities together. All members of the group get absorbed into the experience, everyone joins in. You need that energy to grow and to remove blockages. If things get difficult, a positive attitude will help with that. And when you see an improvement, that is excellent for your self-confidence.

The American National Institute for Play (http://www.nifplay.org/) has done research into the effects of playing and calls play a 'gateway to vitality'.

> *"It generates optimism, seeks out novelty, makes perseverance fun, gives the immune system a bounce, fosters empathy and promotes a sense of belonging and community. A life or culture devoid of or deficient in play exists as a heightened major public health risk factor. The prevalence of depression, stress-related disorders, interpersonal violence, addictions etc. can be linked to the prolonged deprivation of human play.*
>
> *Each person has a unique play personality. When one remains in touch with it, it empowers and brings pleasure to life. Above all, play is fun: it lightens life and makes you feel more optimistic."*

If you're playing with a group of people in a relaxed way, the chances are there will be a lot of spontaneous laughter. That's why children laugh so often, and adults much less so. There are no statistics in terms of numbers, but every adult will have to admit, if they're honest, that they had a lot more fun as a child. I regularly talk to adults who can't remember that last time they laughed. Obviously, that's just incredibly sad.

Stuart Brown, physician, psychiatrist and clinical researcher, is a firm believer in play for adults. During a TED talk in California, he said:

Similarly, laughing is very healthy and improves social interaction. You laugh if you can play, since play unifies. It was a huge revelation for me when I took the laughter workshops. That taught me so much! I took home with me the inspiration and the pleasure of together.

Laughter is fantastic and affects people in wonderful ways. It gives you a brief boost; you experience a high for a short time, but the positive effect lasts for a considerable time afterwards. Laughter has also been proven to be a good medicine for pain. When you laugh, your body produces endorphins, neurotransmitters which reduce pain and are partly responsible for a feeling of well-being and happiness. Laughter has also been shown to be good for your heart and blood vessels. It lowers harmful cholesterol (LDL) and raises healthy cholesterol (HDL).

Our brain does not distinguish between reality and imagination, and neither does our body. The sporting world has long been aware of that and puts it into practice by visualising training sessions. When you think about something fun and positive, you automatically feel happy.

By contrast, when you think about unpleasant events, the effect will be negative; the body responds with stress. So you can determine how you feel to a certain extent. If you have a smile on your face, you feel happier and healthier.

Dr Lee S. Berk, a researcher at Loma Linda University School of Allied Health Professions, has been researching the physical effect of laughter since the 1980s. He and his colleagues were the first to show that daily laughter has a beneficial effect on the hormone system. It ensures that less stress hormones, cortisol and epinephrine are produced. Epinephrine is better known as adrenaline. In addition, when you laugh, the body produces extra white blood cells which strengthen the immune system.

And the following message also shows that laughter is a good medicine for memory loss.

Fight memory loss with a smile   **Date: April 27, 2014**

Source: Federation of American Societies for Experimental Biology (FASEB)

Too much stress can take its toll on the body, mood, and mind. As we age it can contribute to a number of health problems, including high blood pressure, diabetes, and heart disease. Recent research has shown that the stress hormone cortisol damages certain neurons in the brain and can negatively affect memory and learning ability in the elderly. Study co-author and long-time psychoneuroimmunology humor researcher, Dr. Lee Berk, added, "It's simple, the less stress you have the better your memory.

Humor reduces detrimental stress hormones like cortisol that decrease memory hippocampal neurons, lowers your blood pressure, and increases blood flow and your mood state. The act of laughter -- or simply enjoying some humor -- increases the release of endorphins and dopamine in the brain, which provides a sense of pleasure and reward. These positive and beneficial neurochemical changes, in turn, make the immune system function better. There are even changes in brain wave activity towards what's called the "gamma wave band frequency," which also amps up memory and recall. So, indeed, laughter is turning out to be not only a good medicine, but also a memory enhancer adding to our quality of life.

In addition to the beneficial effects on individual health, laughter has a positive effect on the sense of group in particular. If everyone's having fun, the participants find it much easier to interconnect.

Recent studies at the University of Oxford in the UK and Aalto University in Finland have shown that laughing in a group context strengthens social ties. It provides a feeling of pleasure and tranquillity and at the same time, a feeling of safety and closeness.

Social laughter leads to a significant growth in social networks: laughter is infectious and members of a large group who roar with laughter together, produce endorphins at a rapid pace.

The combination of laughing and doing breathing exercises, in Laughter Yoga, has become popular in recent years. There are more than a hundred laughter clubs worldwide. If you know that laughter has such a positive effect on group-forming and ties, it's very clear that you can make use of it in the work environment too. That will have many positive effects. There will be an improvement in the work atmosphere, staff will become enthusiastic, members of the team will become closer, motivation will be strengthened, creativity and innovative impulses increased, and it will help lower stress levels in all active participants. So it's hardly surprising that world-famous Monty Python comedian John Cleese once said, "People who laugh together, work together".

During workshops, I often notice that participants are reluctant to let themselves go; they don't want to laugh. They resist it, because they are too inhibited to just burst into laughter without a reason. They freeze, want to stay in control of the emotions they have hidden away and want to retreat into themselves. They don't dare to reveal the emotions which will be released by the laughter. I can relate to that.

Next to playing and laughing, singing is another thing that has very positive psychological effects. And the strongest effect can be achieved not by singing solo, but by singing songs together with others. An Australian study carried out in 2008 clearly showed that choral singers were even happier than the people in the audience (MacLean). Another study carried out in 1998 showed that the residents of a care home who had sung in a group context for a month were much less anxious and depressed than the residents who had not [ISPS].

Singing is comparable to laughing. Both encourage the production of endorphins, which lift the mood. They also increase the amount of oxygen in the blood and improve circulation, because when you're singing, you have to breathe deeply.

Singing in groups could make you happier, according to new research. Researchers examined the benefits of singing among people with mental health conditions including anxiety and depression. They found that people who took part in a community singing group maintained or improved their mental health. And that the combination of singing and socializing was an essential part of recovery because it promoted an ongoing feeling of belonging and wellbeing.

2017 University of East Anglia /Ecancermedicalscience 2016

Singing in a choir for just one hour boosts levels of immune proteins in people affected by cancer, reduces stress and improves mood, which in turn could have a positive impact on overall health, a new study has found. The study tested 193 members of five different choirs. Results showed that singing for an hour was associated with significant reductions in stress hormones, such as cortisol, and increases in quantities of cytokines -- proteins of the immune system -- which can boost the body's ability to fight serious illness.

The study also found that those with the lowest levels of mental wellbeing and highest levels of depression experienced greatest mood improvement.

Joyful at work

> *The world's greatest innovators exhibit 27 creative attitudes, and playfulness is one of the most critical ones (Kim, 2016).*
>
> *Playfulness lets you approach situations with a sense of humour. You see the situation from a light-hearted point of view and that stimulates a flexible way of thinking.*
>
> *Innovators don't take themselves too seriously. Too much gravity leads to an uncreative and boring life. Innovators are playful, have a good sense of humour and are sometimes even a bit naughty. They demonstrate that play and work can go perfectly well side by side. In fact, play sharpens the curiosity and allows them to step outside their line of thought. This gives them ideas they would otherwise not have had if they had continued to think logically. By stimulating Playfulness, employers stimulate their staff to think up unique solutions and ensure a strengthening of the sense of community. A safe working environment is created in which taking risks is appreciated.*

It can be extremely valuable for companies to introduce *Joyfulness*, of which Playfulness is an element.

You get so much added value when employees work from a sense of *Joy*. As a result, a culture can grow of which creativity and innovation are the main characteristics. Name one company that doesn't want that! If you don't innovate, you will be lagging behind the rest within a few years.

Almost all companies and organisations have the basic conditions in order, a must if a company is to survive. The company or organisation must be viable, and the mission and vision play an important part in this. However, there is a world of difference between these two areas. Terms such as pleasure in work, employee satisfaction, culture, image, communication and management structure are, of course, well-known as is 'Socially-responsible entrepreneurship'.

Taking *Joyfulness* into consideration, programmes have been developed which connect all the important organisational elements with each other. Important factors in that are focus on pressure of work and pleasure in work, creativity and innovation. I firmly believe that a rational approach alone is not enough. Many things take place in companies and organisations which cannot be explained from a purely rational perspective. Much occurs at an energy level between individuals, between teams or departments and between staff and management. It's precisely by obtaining insight into the relationships and beliefs of all the players involved in the company that you can continue to develop. Organisational development is very similar to personal growth, and a Company Constellation is very similar to a Family Constellation. By experiencing things intuitively, you become aware of what is going on.

Companies will perform much better if they have employees who are creative and enjoy doing their part for the company mission. And companies will realise that investing in *Joyfulness* achieves more than any brainstorming session ever did. Devising and setting up new rules and protocols has little effect, since it's a one-sided action based on mistrust. Here too, you could get a better balance between intuition and reason. *Joyfulness* in your company is like the bubbles in the champagne; it ensures that staff are motivated and enjoy coming to work. It will also strengthen the company's image in a positive sense.

The challenge for companies is to deploy staff based on their individual talent. That means offering much more scope for individual qualities and making full use of the talent present. For staff it means a chance to be themselves and show what they can do. They consequently take more pleasure in their work and that in turn leads to a reduction in stress and less sick leave.

Teams benefit too. We have already mentioned the advantages. In short, they consist of an increase in creativity, a strengthening of the teamwork, improved communication and social interaction and more self-reliance and independence.

And yet only a very few companies dare to implement this play culture. Naturally, running a company is a serious business; profits must be made and risks limited. That's logical: you have to survive in a constantly changing market. But without product development and innovative solutions, you won't make it in the long term. And that goes not only for companies, but also for government, semi-public agencies and other social organisations.

Until now, knowledge and application of a 'play culture' in companies was rare. Strangely enough, companies often view play as the opposite of work. If you're playing, you're not working and if you're working, you don't play.

A great many limiting beliefs are in the way here:

- It would be nice to be able to play more, but I'm here to work.

- I don't have time for that, there's more than enough work to be done.

- Play is for children. Adults don't play.

Precisely in a time when society is becoming more complex, due in part to an increasing barrage of information, *Joyfulness* could offer a worthwhile contribution to business operations. It could be as simple as a separate activity in the lunch break, as with company fitness. Naturally, that's not enough. The trick is to enable staff to do their work in a playful way. It doesn't all have to be organised in such a weighty and serious fashion. That kind of tight managements is only aimed at keeping staff under control. It's a system based on distrust and it hinders innovation. That's why it's better to improve inner pleasure and remove the pressure. It's time for corporate joyfulness!

Unfortunately, there are many organisations in which promoting inner pleasure and removing pressure can be quite a challenge. Social safety at work is crucial if staff are to be innovative. Yet ten percent of employed people in the Netherlands does not experience that safety. Hassles, bullying, power-hungry bosses and uncooperative colleagues are all too common, a consequence of the idea that the other person is a competitor and based on the old adage: knowledge is power. In such a situation, who would dare to stick their neck out? Who would dare to put forward a fresh new idea?

Every organisation benefits from staff who genuinely cooperate. From people who share knowledge in the hope that it will benefit the other. Bundling unique qualities leads to new insights and that is only possible if the whole competitive nonsense disappears. Organisations need to start appreciating and rewarding employees for working together to achieve a result. A culture of sharing is the precondition for innovative solutions.

You will see an even deeper cooperation when people work from mutual compassion. Showing compassion at work is hugely important, for both staff and management. It's about being aware that someone else needs your attention. About sincerely showing understanding for someone else's personal circumstances and actually doing something to ease or improve the situation.

The importance of compassion as an asset to an organisation has been clearly demonstrated. People work better together because they feel respected and trusted. There is less absence due to stress, less sick leave, more pleasure in work and increased productivity, financial results are better, customer satisfaction increases and there is a greater capacity for innovation.

In recent years, more and more companies have embraced the Lean method, which involved constant improvement of processes revolving around the customer. In this system, a company's staff are of great value and it's important that they are happy. They are given the opportunity of thinking about improvements to the work and to collaboration.

I personally thoroughly enjoyed using the Lean method during my time as a manager. The margin within which you must operate is predetermined, but other than that, staff are given lots of scope to come up with suggestions for improvements. They work towards a daring goal. The nice thing is that management assumes that neither the goal nor the path towards it are yet entirely clear; after all, you can't know everything beforehand. Because you are given scope to apply your creativity, new ideas and future possibilities occur along the way. The path to the goal is one big organic movement. The play organisation culture I envisage with *Joyfulness* would be a wonderful addition to this method. Allowing and promoting play is beneficial to creativity and leads to an atmosphere in which making proposals is not strange at all, even if they are uncommon in nature. It's precisely the introduction of unusual and original ideas that provides innovative power.

It means that staff can identify with the organisation's mission and vision and are allowed to influence them, based on *Joy*. It's not a mission or vision which management has drawn up, but rather a goal to which staff can make their own unique contribution. They know that their input will get them a little closer to reaching the goal. That realisation will get them working with heart and soul: the combination of personal involvement in the goal and the unique individual input will make all the difference. It gets staff and organisation on the same page, something that management cannot force by way of rules or protocol, which do not motivate. An employee needs to feel that their work is meaningful, otherwise the mission will not be effective. ''Joyfulness at work' could make that happen.

If one can work in a relaxed and joyful atmosphere, one can enhance work efficiency and ease work pressure. Playfulness benefits not only children's growth but also adults' psychological and physical balance; therefore, a society with playfulness is highly valued and receives its importance. Furthermore, playfulness at work can alleviate boredom, release tensions and inspire creativity. In a playfulness climate, one would devote oneself to work with high internal motivation, which enhances enjoyment, involvement, and satisfaction. Consequently, it is suggested to incorporate playfulness finely in work to increase one's pleasure and involvement at work, and to develop employee playfulness to catalyse breakthrough and potential.

Playfulness and Innovation--A Multilevel Study in Individuals and Organizations Department of International Business, National Kaohsiung University of Applied Sciences, Kaohsiung, Taiwan

Learning should be a joy

Learning ... should be a joy and full of excitement.

It is life's greatest adventure

It is an illustrated excursion into the minds of noble and learned men

not a conducted tour through a jail.

Taylor Caldwell 1957

This part of the book is illustrated by a Picasso painting. The playful and joyful energy of youth positively flies off the canvas, which makes it so sad when you realise that the focus of youth is so firmly fixed on reasoning, competition and performance. The young hold the future, but which future? What kind of life do we want to give our children? Do we really want our children to still be as performance-oriented twenty years from now? Do we really want to see our children so stressed that they can no longer enjoy doing anything? The consequence will be that they will suffer burn-out early in their adult lives; that they don't know who they are and at thirty, still don't know what they want to be.

I don't believe this is something any parent wants for their children. And I assume that teachers want to spare their students this fate. Surely we must now realise how restrictive this performance-oriented thinking is? And we're saddling our children with it. Let's not do this anymore. Let's stop grooming our children for a society which makes people ill. Let's stop expressing everything in results and numbers, simply to fuel competition among people. Let's make it clear that work and play go together, and that creativity and intuition are every bit as important as reasoning. Expressing unique qualities in numbers is madness.

I read an article written in 2017 by education advisor Martine Blonk-Meulenkamp, on the website wij-leren.nl. In it, she wonders how we can stimulate creativity in children in education. Creativity is largely neglected in the current system, which consists of ninety percent rationality and ten percent creativity. Martine Blonk-Meulenkamp believes that a balance of fifty-fifty would be much better. I quote:

"Our children need creative education. The focus at school should move from rationality to intuition/creativity. That means making a radical change in our thinking on the idea of 'school'. In that case, education would not be about rational matters such as curriculum, teaching methods or results. We want to help children along in their own development which is why the core of our education lies in responding to children's gifts and ways of thinking. Rationality has a supporting role in this and should be applied servant. That way, a balance will be achieved between intuition/creativity and rationality.

And that's what we all want: inquisitive students who go searching of their own accord for that which we want to achieve rationally in our education system. But how do we stimulate this attitude in children? As a teacher, you have to start with yourself: do you indeed find development of intuition/creativity important for children (and adults) and are you prepared to adjust your teaching accordingly?"

I'm so happy to see an educator writing this, and I couldn't agree more. It gives me hope that changes will take place. Let's please allow our children to be children at school; let them experience that things are most enjoyable when done together. Incorporate it into the lessons. What could be nicer than playing and creating things together, particularly if you know that it's also healthy and promotes creativity? And encourage young children to do those activities outside the classroom too, so that they get some fresh air. Let children create something together which makes them all happy. That will provide the energy every child needs to develop personally. While playing, they get to know themselves and discover that it's okay to be yourself, with all your quirks. Those same quirks may well later turn out to be your gifts.

Children should dance more at school. That's much more beneficial than gym lessons, according to researchers at the University of Helsinki. They recommended that dancing be included in the Finnish curriculum.

The compulsory gym lessons are a horror for many pupils. They dislike the competitive element and experience pressure to prove who is the best. The ArtsEqual Research Initiative, coordinated by the University of the Arts in Helsinki, discovered however that forms of physical exercise which allow more freedom of expression, such as dancing, do in fact appeal to children.

According to the Finnish research, dancing combines physical exercise with expressing emotions, social interaction and cultural participation. So dancing would not only contribute to the physical health of children and teenagers but would also improve mental health and a sense of community. In addition, it stimulates learning achievements.

Nu.nl 24 februari 2019

Martine Blonk-Meulenkamp calls on educators to rebel against the predominant education culture in which the focus is mainly on rationality and in which financial considerations are a priority. She hopes a real change will take place, since today's society needs creative, flexible thinkers.

In a very popular TED talk in 2006, education expert Sir Ken Robson said that schools kill creativity. Children no longer develop their creativity; the education system stems it. His assertion is: "We get educated out of it". In the follow-up TED talk presentation in 2010, he said:

> *I meet all kinds of people who don't enjoy what they do. They simply go through their lives getting on with it. They get no great pleasure from what they do. They endure it rather than enjoy it, and wait for the weekend. How many people do you know that go through/endure life this way? Are you one of them? If you are, you're not in the minority, no, unfortunately you are in the majority. Is this in part because of the education system? Maybe, but I also feel it is a case of how we have been conditioned over many generations.*

It's time to change that conditioning: "If enough people take action, you have a movement and if the movement has enough energy, you have a revolution." I couldn't agree more. It's high time we put an end to the existing competitive, performance-oriented conditioning which starts at school.

But we haven't yet heard from the children themselves. How do they feel about this? They were given an opportunity to say what they need from school during the children's rights tour by the Children's Ombudsman in 2016. The children felt that there could be less pressure on work and performance.

The Children's Ombudsman on the children's rights tour - 'If you ask us'. 2016, December.

Our conclusions:

1. Real attention

Children and young people need real attention from the people around them; parents, family and friends and also professionals. That means showing interest, taking time, listening attentively and seeing the child as a person.

By way of rounding off the theme of education, one last lesson; a lesson in 'Living in the here and now'. Children are very good at doing that.

The mission of the Joyfulness Worldwide Cooperative is to create a world in which all humans stay connected to their natural state of Joy.

Will you make the difference?

We heard earlier about some inspiring examples of people who put their passion into doing something unique. They used it for a personal mission. Everyone potentially has that power, but it's sometimes hidden deep inside. If you can tap into it, there is nothing more wonderful than committing your unique 'Being' and your unique talent to realising a mission, creating something unique or doing something meaningful for others. On your own or together. That's working from *Joyfulness*. It's like the saying 'working with heart and soul'. If you use this power, work is no longer work and giving is no longer giving.

> *Work is love made visible. And if you cannot work with love but only with distaste, it is better that you should leave your work and sit at the gate of the temple and take alms of those who work with joy.*
>
> **Kahlil Gibran**

Who wouldn't want to work from passion and enthusiasm? You'll discover that you can have that unique feeling of *Joyfulness* when you're at work too. At such moments, everything converges; you are appreciated for your talent and work becomes an interesting challenge. You get to work with enthusiasm and love and results come of their own accord.

When you have a sound basis and a life based on *Joy,* you feel strong and self-confident. You don't need approval from others because you're holding your own. You feel alive and decisive, you're proud of who you are, you dare to be yourself and be heard and you connect with others.

If you dare to live a life which suits you personally, it doesn't matter what other people think of you, which allows you to let go of the never-ending 'having to'. 'Being' and 'having to' don't go together. 'Having to' disturbs the flow, as does pressure to perform.

You will be happiest in your life if you are doing things passionately and with pleasure. This in turn will give you more self-confidence based on play. You will grow in your work and be increasingly better at expressing yourself in a way which fully suits you. Intuition and rationality become balanced and this allows you to live, work and play with others. You can be yourself, without having to achieve in areas which are really not suitable for you. Passion is combining that which you are good at with that which you enjoy. There's nothing greater than doing that which is completely in line with your feeling of *Joy.* And this is expressed in the way you communicate, collaborate and create things. If your passion has become your work, it will no longer feel like work but more like a personal creation.

> *There is no greater joy nor greater reward than to make a fundamental difference in someone's life.*
>
> Mary Rose McGeady

You may well have developed your inner passion and personal strength, but the question is what to do next. Where will you direct your inner *Joy*? What will you change in your surroundings? How will you present yourself to others? With whom will you connect? What will inspire you? What are your most important motives? What do you see as your mission?

It took me long time to feel free enough to show my real self and what my passion is. I'm intuitive and sensitive and I know or see things which most people cannot understand. For a very long time, I didn't dare to show who I really am and adapted too much to my surroundings. Not only in my private life; I also had to survive at work. That meant keeping the real Johan from myself and others.

Thankfully, the times have changed. I am now a member of a professional organisation, as an Energy Therapist. My consultations are often covered by your health insurance, depending on the type of policy you have. I have experienced a huge growth in recent years and am now pretty unaffected by what other people think of me. I know who I am, what my talents are and how I can use them to help others. Naturally, I know I also have limitations; I absolutely recognise that with my perception and vision, I only see or know a part of the reality. That's also true for what I have written in this book. That too may only be a part of the reality. Despite that, I want to share with you my story, experience and vision. It comes straight from my heart. Who knows, maybe I can make a difference in my own way?

To make a difference in someone's life you don't have to be brilliant, rich, beautiful or perfect.

You just have to care.

Mandy Hale Read

Of course, not everyone has to create something. Not everyone is a creator or a doer. Not being a creator does not in any way make you inferior to others. For that reason, I make a distinction between compassion and creation. Neither is better than or inferior to the other. Both are expressions of enjoyment and energy. In fact, you can manifest simply by being there for others, from the heart. This is also a way of making a difference.

How will you make a difference?

It starts with a Spark!

Through my quest for happiness, I have found my personal mission. I had to go through dark periods, and I was mercilessly confronted by my boundaries. That was painful, but I learned such a lot from it. I know what stress is. I also experienced a burn-out on my journey. I thought building a career was important and forgot who I really am, deep inside. There was a time when that made me feel lonely and misunderstood. Of course, I actually brought that on myself, because I didn't dare to reveal the real Johan.

Now I know that you can change everything. You can find your own power and *Joy* even if you've been knocked out completely. In my case, it was clearly about making the decision to choose to be who I really am, deep inside. To no longer allow myself to be governed by what others think of me or expect from me. And now I'm able to fully enjoy the fact that I am living based on my feelings and intuition. I absolutely love being able to direct my energy at creating something wonderful and meeting people who share in that. My experience recently has been that even miracles can happen. I find it inconceivable that I have rediscovered how it feels to be happy.

The things that have happened in my life have led to me finding my mission.

I wish everyone could experience this journey of discovery. Too many people are being destroyed by having to perform under pressure, the effects of competition and the accompanying stress. Many young people who have only just started a job have no idea who they really are, deep inside. Since they are predominantly using their heads, they are unable to access their hearts. They don't understand why they're so unhappy, when they appear to have everything. However, their focus is too much on 'becoming' someone, rather than just 'being' someone. It's what they've been taught. It would be fantastic if they could feel their Spark again. They all actually have the potential to function based on their unique 'Being', to feel and radiate *Joy.*

> *A Joyful life is an individual creation*
>
> *that cannot be copied from a recipe.*
>
> Mihaly Csikszentmihalyi

My mission is to show others how we are interacting in this society. I can't just sit back and watch as we allow ourselves to be governed almost solely by reasoning, performance and economic drive. We are damaging children with it from an early age because we are pressurising them to perform and that causes them a lot of stress. Also, it's quite unacceptable that ten percent of people are bullied by colleagues at work. Or that fifteen percent of people in employment has a burn-out or is on the brink of one.

I firmly believe that viewing such excesses as abnormal, and criticising them, is very healthy. But if you talk the talk, you have to walk the walk. Talking without taking action will not change anything. So we're going to do something about this. Not on our own, but together!

Let's combine our *Joy* and inspire others with it.

It starts with a Spark.

It's time for *Joyfulness* to brighten our world!

Joyfulness references

This is not the umpteenth self-help book. For that reason, I have included no exercises, assignments, visualisation or meditations.

As far as I'm concerned, there are more than enough books on sale where all this can be found. Another such book would add nothing extra. There are plenty of methods you can use to meditate on a cushion on your own, at home. *Joyfulness* doesn't concern just you alone! There is enough individuality in the world.

My message is about the importance of *Together*. About how you can feel and build up *Joy* together, in play, and spread it throughout the world. Because *Joy* will only catch on if you have others around you, at home, at work or at school. *Joy* is all about the interaction between you and the other person. You give and receive without judgement, but with compassion.

Discovering, experiencing and being able to share your *Joy* is often a difficult process. You will have to say goodbye to all manner of limiting beliefs which are getting in the way of your *Joy*. However, that is a unique process; the approach cannot be described in a book, and certainly not with the aid of standard exercises. Your unique situation requires a personal approach and tailored supervision. The best thing to do is to find a good coach or supervisor who works intuitively.

Check the website for a list of consultants, workshops, training courses and personal coaching offered by trainers and coaches affiliated with Joyfulness® (www.joyfulness.world).

For the sake of clarity, I have summarised the most important reference sources mentioned in this book.

Joyfulness arises when you are your authentic self and from that feeling, you connect with other people.

As a result of this connection, there will be a feeling of happiness because you give, receive and let it be.

So it's a happy state of 'Being'.

Don't make Joy and personal happiness a goal in itself; it occurs through 'Being' and not through 'becoming'.

Get in touch with your inner child. Go and have fun, explore, play, dance, laugh together with others, in a group. It will give everyone extra energy.

Set a higher goal for yourself, based on human and social commitment. Ask yourself how you want to use your Joy to make a difference.

Be guided by your mission and trust that the right people and events will cross your path.

Don't fall into the trap of competition and pressure to perform and don't forget to think about things and keep playing; that way you will grow naturally from Joy towards your goal.

You'll notice that you automatically get a lot of energy if you stick to your 'Being' and the accompanying goal.

Give without having to get anything in return.

Live and work based on compassion; follow your heart.

Don't take any notice of other people's opinions or judgement. This is your unique life.

Open yourself to your intuition. Let yourself be amazed by the information and ideas which spring to mind at unexpected moments when you stop looking rationally for solutions.

Dispose of all beliefs which get in the way of Joy. Start with a personal clearing out if necessary and get a coach to help you if you can't manage it alone.

Celebrate life by being yourself and being there for others.

Let yourself be seen and heard.

Live a Joyful life!

And most importantly: live together Joyfully!

Epilogue

I'd like to go back to the personal stories in this book about my child, K. K stands for the Dutch word 'kind', meaning child. I don't mention any real names due to privacy considerations. The situation at present, though still not ideal, is slightly better than it was. That is thanks to the efforts of many practitioners, in particular, and certainly to my ex-wife. They are all still working hard to keep the situation stable. I admire that so much. They keep going because K is a beautiful child and I agree, of course, but I have distanced myself a bit.

And whatever happens, or whatever is going to happen, loving each other is always the best thing you can do. That's certainly true of my love for K. Luckily, things are going well with my other daughters too. They are adventurous and both go happily through life relying on their heads and their hearts. As a father, that's wonderful to see.

Joyfulness Cooperative

The Joyfulness Cooperative was founded in the Netherlands, in June 2019, by independent entrepreneurs who together apply and radiate *Joyfulness*.

The cooperative operates internationally. Entrepreneurs from all corners of the world can become members, with the Dutch cooperative as a central body. Anyone can become a Friend and support the Joyfulness Movement.

Joyfulness® is a registered trademark with worldwide protection.

The participating entrepreneurs contribute their expertise to a world which works and lives based on *Joyfulness*, a world in which *Joy*, compassion, creativity and intuition are clearly visible.

They advise and/or coach private individuals, businesses and organisations and care and education institutions in the setting up and maintenance of a *Joyfulness*® working and living environment.

They organise meetings, training sessions and workshops.

They carry out work or activities which contribute to feeling and radiating *Joyfulness*.

They demonstrate and express *Joy*.

A part of the profits from the cooperative goes to support distinctive *Joyfulness* projects throughout the world. Donations in support of these projects are very welcome.

For more information about the cooperative, the entrepreneurs taking part, the activities and the projects, go to www.joyfulness.world

If you would like to use your talent to contribute to there being more *Joy* in the world, please get in touch with us for a personal interview.

Word of thanks

In the first place, of course, I would like to thank my wife, Margreeth van Eersel. She inspires me every day with her warmth and *Joy*. She was talking about my book before I even planned on writing it.

I would also like to thank my father, Matthijs Spaans, who died in 2014. He is still encouraging me, from his 'other world'.

I would also like to mention the first people who offered feedback: Marike Vroom, Ineke van Eersel, Dine-Marij Roeterd, Circe Simons, Haley Berghuis, Cora Reurings, Monique Willemsen, Lonneke Messelink.

And thanks to Jan Beenen, himself very *Joyful*, for the final editing of the book.

I would like to thank Lizzie Kean for translating this book from Dutch during the heat of the summer months. www.lizziekean.nl

Thanks also to Carianne van Raak for her creative contribution to the book cover and the website. www.cariannevanraak.nl

Rob Otterspeer (robreclame@hotmail.nl) is responsible for the beautiful illustration of *Andere Wereld*. I can't wait to see his children's book and the amazing illustrations.

Trainers Sander Wisse, Gerrit Menting and Annemiek Hormann, of the IMC Mensontwikkeling programme Intuitive Coaching, inspired me greatly.

A special word of thanks to coach Titia Kroep and supervisor Leila van Veen of ABGL. They have been a great support. www.abgl.nl

Lydia Knoop took the beautiful portrait photos for the book, the cover and the website, and she also took my portrait photo. She gives the soul a voice in her photos. www.lydiaknoop.com

About the author

Johan was born in The Hague in 1959. He graduated in Social Geography from the Free University of Amsterdam and went on to work for a time as a staff member/advisor with the PvdA (left-wing political party) faction in Parliament. In the ensuing twenty years, he held a number of management positions, such as head of a social security office, manager of Public Affairs, manager of Internal Services and Programme Manager of Organisation Development.

Johan and Margreeth are the proprietors of the company *Andere Wereld* in Welsum.

Johan has a naturopathy practice, working as an Energy Therapist, and is a member of the LVNG (Dutch National Association of Naturopaths).

Johan is also an Intuition coach and certified Stress and Burn-out coach.

Both Margreeth and Johan are Laughter Yoga teachers and *Andere Wereld is* a place in which to find tranquillity. There are two oriental-style holiday homes with sauna on the grounds, and a Lapland fire hut in the garden. www.eenanderewereld.nl

In 2019, Margreeth and Johan founded the Joyfulness Cooperation U.A., aimed at making an active contribution, together with other independent entrepreneurs, to a world which offers more scope for *Joy*, compassion, creation and intuition.

Johan is often invited as a guest speaker. For more information about this and other activities:

www.johanspaans.nl

Source acknowledgements

Als je het mij vraagt. De Kinderombudsman Report, December 2016.

Understanding Creative Intuition. Theresa Hardman, www.academia.edu

De vergeten gave van creativiteit. Martine Blonk-Meulenkamp, 2017, www.wij-leren.nl

Various scientific studies, www.sciencedaily.com

Andrew Johnson, PhD Minnesota State University, Mankato, www.opdt-johnson.com

Carl Rogers on Creativity, www.psychologytoday.com

Het pad van de Inca. Prenella Sami, Uitgeverij Petiet, 2009.

Handboek coachen bij stress en burn-out. Annita Rogier, Boom 2017

Darwin was geen Darwinist. Carel Peeters, Vrij Nederland, 2009, www.vn.nl

www.pursuit-of-happiness.org

www.collective-evolution.com

www.vtv2018.nl/druk-op-jongeren

www.iederkindeentalent.nl

www.ombir.org

www.nifplay.org

www.intermediair.nl

www.youtube.com about Nick Vujicic

www.oudersvannu.nl (magazine for parents)

"